Understand your relationship— and what you can do to improve it!

Save your marriage, rescue a faltering relationship, find out whether your partner loves you, if your love can last forever, and more! Developed by a practicing psychotherapist with over thirty years of clinical experience and renowned for his successful psychological tests, *The Love Test* helps define the magic of romance, reveals what is happening in *your* relationship, and tells you how to make it the love of your dreams.

"This is the best book since Masters and Johnson to give couples basic information for a successful love relationship."

—Ralph L. Miller, Th.M., Ph.D.
Professor of Counselor Education,
San Diego State University

HAROLD BESSELL, Ph.D. is the father of the Bessell Measurement of Emotional Maturity Scales, an instrument that meets the standards of the American Psychological Association and is widely used to measure the emotional maturity of children. The questionnaires and methods in *The Love Test* grew out of the author's clinical research and testing of thousands of students and an over thirty-year practice with over forty thousand counseling sessions. The emotional maturity test in this book is based on his earlier, highly successful test for children.

The Love Test

HAROLD BESSELL, Ph.D.

WARNER BOOKS

A Warner Communications Company

This book is affectionately and gratefully dedicated
to my wife, Pat, who first awakened in me
the experience of romantic excitement
and then, with patient persistence,
showed me the caring that makes it all work.
It was her unremitting faith
and her challenge to respond in kind
that taught me what love is all about.

*While the case histories in this book represent real people, in all
instances the names and identifying material have been changed to
protect their privacy.*

Cover design by David Gatti

Warner Books, Inc.
666 Fifth Avenue
New York, N.Y. 10103

 A Warner Communications Company

Printed in the United States of America

First Warner Books Printing: March, 1985

10 9 8 7 6 5 4 3 2 1

Preface

This book has not been written by chance. In many ways it is my personal story and the story of those whose lives I have touched closely. Yet, there is a common thread in all our lives. It is the need for meaning, for satisfying involvement with other people, people who are like us in many ways and yet who provide an almost infinite variety of possible interactions.

At our core we are *people* people. We need each other, and the success or failure in life for each of us is the extent to which our involvements with people have been mostly satisfying, fulfilling, enriching experiences, or if they have been empty, disappointing, and frustrating.

As I look back over my years, my most joyous experiences have been those in which there was a rich, close, and meaningful interaction with another person. As a child I was essentially innocent, passive, the lucky beneficiary of good experiences and the unfortunate victim of unpleasant encounters. I was inexperienced and helpless. It was mostly a matter of chance, of luck. But as I became more experienced, more aware, I learned that to a large extent I could indeed become the master of my fate. As an adult, it could and should be much more a matter of knowing who I am, what I am, and what I need for a good life. One saying goes, "We grow too soon old, and too late smart."

The wisdom I have earned through both pleasure and pain is that there is a second chance for all of us. The key lies in knowing that we can influence our destinies, and that the happiest destinies are those in which we

pursue our lives in the secure and exciting companionship of another human being whom we know, trust,
respect, and enjoy. The challenge for all of us is to find
one of the many possible companions who feels the
same about us as we do about them. While choice is not
everything, it is the first step. The next step is to work
at bringing out the best in each other every day of our
lives.

In my youth I blundered along until one day I was
very lucky. And because what I experienced with my
wife of now twenty-nine years was so new, so different,
so incomprehensible, I almost passed it by. But fate
does not need to be dictated by luck. Through knowing
what it is that you need the very most, you will
immeasurably increase your chances of finding a fulfilling companion *for you*, or of building your present
relationship into a much more satisfying, mutually rewarding one.

This book is intended to help you better understand
what makes a fulfilling romantic relationship, and to
help you avoid the common pitfalls that bring misery to
so many. However, no book can possibly deal completely
with such a thing as individual personality.

A book is a form of one-way communication. You are
unique and your relationship is therefore unique, with
its own complexities. I cannot emphasize enough how
much you owe it to yourself, and to your partner,
therefore, to consult a professional counselor if, after
reading and using the materials in this book, you consider a major change in your life or your relationship.

—H.B.
La Jolla, California

Acknowledgments

Thanks to my wife, Pat, for her support from the very beginning to the very end of the task of preparing this book, for having read and reread each successive refinement of the manuscript, for her insightful suggestions, and for making everything easier by being the loving partner that writing a book such as this requires.

Thanks also to those who believed in me and encouraged me: my sons, Tim and Peter, for their help in the research on measuring maturity; my daughter, Katherine, for her wise and most constructive critical guidance; my agent, Margaret McBride, for her undaunted enthusiasm; my editor, Pat Golbitz, for her instantaneous recognition of the significance of this new approach to the diagnosis of the romantic relationship; Michael Gershman for his help in historical case histories. Thanks also to Dr. Vincent E. Mazzanti, Dr. Barbara Rosen, Peggy Chana, and Eva Hough, for reading and giving their many helpful and valuable criticisms to the manuscript; to Dawn Rawls for her careful editorial assistance and suggestions; and Sharon Fleming for her proofing and typing of the final manuscript.

Special thanks also to the editorial staff at Apple Tree Productions in Los Angeles who produced this book.

Contents

Contents

Chapter One

♡ ♡ ♡

The Most Important Personal Decision of Your Life

Choosing the right love partner is the most important personal decision in your life. Love may make the world go around, but if you are married to the wrong partner, love can make you pretty miserable.

Thirty years as a psychotherapist and more than forty thousand counseling sessions have taught me a great deal about love. Probably half of those persons who have married, have married for the wrong reasons. A great many of these people remain together, wistfully hoping for better, or struggling to make an unfulfilling, difficult relationship work. Many couples finally separate or divorce after living frustrating lives together. And perhaps as many as fifty percent of those who do get divorced may have divorced for the wrong reasons!

How much of this misery and wasted effort could have been prevented?

Unhappy romantic relationships run rampant and marriage counselors are needed. However, the popularity of counseling is not so much the result of increased suffering as it is the demand for better education. Many

1

more people today are aware that there is much to *learn* about making a relationship work and that, through education and understanding, a relationship may be improved. More spouses, partners, and lovers are determined to discover what is required for happy, healthy living and loving.

Few of us are prepared through school or our families to recognize the difference between genuine romantic interest, which lasts a very long time, and infatuation, which is often fleeting. One research finding shows that six out of seven romances fall apart within a few short months. National statistics tell us that six out of every ten marriages will fail. Other couples marry, discover they have made a mistake, and remain together unhappily.

For a very long time, marriage has been a gamble for practically everyone. But it is far too important a decision to be left to chance, especially now that we know better how to predict the future of a love relationship.

In this book you have a road map and a compass with which you can direct yourself through the delightful but often treacherous woods of romantic involvement. If you are presently involved with someone, then it is critically important for you to find out if you might be separating for the wrong reasons, or remaining together for the wrong reasons. I will put the tools, The Love Test, in your hands and will show you how to use them. The rest is up to you.

The Love Test

The Love Test is comprised of two tools of measurement you will need to gain a better understanding of your love relationship. These tests have been developed from my experiences with the many patients who have come to me seeking help.

Over the past thirty years I have used a wide variety of projective and paper-and-pencil tests. During the 1970's I set out to develop an instrument that would measure, on the basis of observation, the emotional

TYPES OF
LOVE RELATIONSHIPS

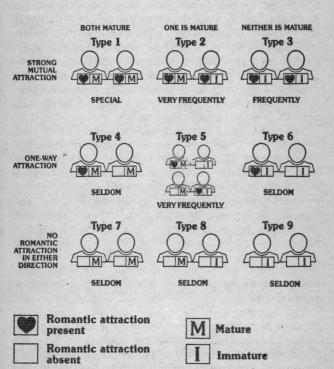

The Love Relationships Chart shows the nine basic types of relationships possible when considering the factors of romantic attraction and emotional maturity.

No relationship will fit neatly into any one category, but the chart is intended as a guide to help you see which category your relationship most closely resembles.

maturity of children between the ages of five and eleven. This instrument meets the standards of the American Psychological Association and is called the Bessell Measurement of Emotional Maturity Scales. The Emotional Maturity Rating Form (EMRF)—one of the two parts of The Love Test—is my adaptation of the 237 items on the Bessell Measurement of Emotional Maturity Scales. Experience in my practice and with my students at the Extension Division of the University of California at San Diego has shown that this sixty-three-item test is sufficient to make a satisfactory assessment of one's love partner for the sake of diagnosing emotional maturity as it affects the love relationship. While the EMRF is not a standardized test, it is derived from a scientific instrument.

Ten years ago I began to combine the EMRF with another quiz, one that measures romantic attraction. The Romantic Attraction Questionnaire (RAQ) is a sentiment scale, a very personal tool that attempts to measure feelings. It measures only *your* feelings.

The Romantic Attraction Questionnaire is not and should not be considered a standardized "objective" test. In the professional sense, it is not even a test but rather a sentiment scale. What is being measured is personal taste. The items of the RAQ represent statements made by my clients over the past thirty years while describing how they felt about their romantic relationships.

The Emotional Maturity Rating Form attempts to measure a broad spectrum of behavior and is a somewhat different kind of measuring instrument. It is like the RAQ in the sense that ratings are being made by an interested, very emotionally involved party in the relationship. You rate your partner's, not your own, behavior in each of four different categories: awareness, relating, competence, and integrity.

When both partners have scored the scales, the scores can be put into your Personal Love Profile (p. 102). Your Personal Love Profile will show which of nine different, basic types of relationships yours most closely resembles. Then you can refer to the Love Relationships Chart which follows to get a clearer picture of the various strengths and weaknesses in your relationship.

What Is Love?

Throughout time, each man and woman has had his or her own opinion of what love is, and isn't. All the definitions are totally subjective. Paul Popenoe, a marriage counselor with extensive experience, said, "Love is a mysterious visitation, which comes out of nowhere into the here and takes hold of you—just like the measles." A man unhappy in love, André Maurois, said, "We owe to the Middle Ages the two worst inventions of humanity—romantic love and gunpowder."

I've found that love is a combination of two separate but equally important parts: romantic love, or "chemistry," and emotional maturity. These two elements together make for the lasting true love of which we all dream. When these two separate elements are combined in improper or unequal portions, they make for unhappy love affairs, miserable marriages, and divorce statistics. The required degree of romantic attraction and of emotional maturity simply must be present in both partners. One-way love is unrequited love.

Romantic attraction is an invisible force, like magnetism, gravity, and electricity. You can't see it, you can't touch it, you can't smell it, but you recognize it by its effects. Romantic attraction cannot be created, because it's a biopsychological force, relating to each individual's ability to be attracted to another specific individual. It is not necessarily reciprocated; there are no rules or reasons that explain its existence. I may be attracted to Mary; John has no interest in Mary other than to note she's a very nice person. Mary may or may not be attracted to me, or to John. Romantic attraction is either there or not there. And if it's real, it will last forever. We do not know how to create romantic attraction nor do we know how to remove it.

Emotional maturity, on the other hand, is a very different aspect of true love. Maturity can always be improved and enriched. You can never be *too* mature. Luckily for all of us, we may begin in a relationship as immature individuals and can improve that relationship by gaining maturity. So before you break up for the wrong reasons (and perhaps as many as half of the people who divorce do so for the wrong reasons), you owe it to yourself to discover if your maturity problem can be overcome and your relationship improved.

Romantic Attraction or Infatuation?

Many of the people who divorce have been the victims of infatuation. They married in haste, often without enough experience to be able to tell the difference between true love and infatuation. True love and infatuation can feel identical in the early stages. They both produce the same kind of high scores on the Romantic Attraction Questionnaire.

There is one big, all-important difference. Those wonderful feelings that tell you this person was made for you don't last with infatuation. With true love, the feelings not only last but can deepen.

The more you get to know someone, the more you are able to judge the difference between fantasy and reality. When you are seeing someone daily, your fantasies end as you learn more and more about each other. And once the fantasies begin to end, the excitement is turned off, the bubble bursts, and the romance begins to fade. The infatuation period ends. Sometimes the affair is over in a few days or weeks, but research shows that, six times out of seven, the romantic interest turns out to be infatuation rather than true romantic attraction.

Infatuation will *probably* wear off in 90 to 120 days if the partners in the love match see each other as often as possible and really get to know each other. This means they should spend as much time as possible with each other (without moving in together!)—perhaps two or three times during the week and many weekends. With this much time together, the excitement will wear thin around the edges by the third or fourth month. If your feelings don't weaken after this much time together, it looks like you've got romantic attraction on your side.

INFATUATION OR TRUE ROMANTIC CHEMISTRY? SIMILARITIES AND DIFFERENCES

Infatuation	*True Romantic Attraction*
Similarities	
Initially strong feelings of pleasurable excitement	Initially strong feelings of pleasurable excitement
Strong desire to be with that person	Strong desire to be with that person
You may or may not like, trust, or respect this person	You may or may not like, trust, or respect this person
High scores on Romantic Attraction Questionnaire	High scores on Romantic Attraction Questionnaire
Not related to emotional maturity of either person	Not related to emotional maturity of either person
Differences	
Based on limited time and real association	Lasts more than three or four months, usually indefinitely
A fantasy trip based on your wishes	Reality, based on genuine attraction and long-continuing satisfaction with the companionship of this person
The sexual interest weakens	The sexual interest persists
Real and frequent contact breaks the spell	Real and frequent contact reinforces the "chemical" attraction whether you like, trust, and respect the person or not

Infatuation	True Romantic Attraction
When the relationship ends, it is over forever, and you feel enlightened, relieved	The attraction of the other person's personality usually lasts indefinitely, whether or not you like, trust, or respect this person
The desire for association ends, a case of "mistaken identity"	The desire for association remains indefinitely
Strong emotion triggered by wish-fulfilling fantasy	Strong emotion as a normal positive biopsychological sense of excitement that is an intrinsic response not based upon or continued by fantasy
Almost always starts immediately, and ends soon	Though often starts immediately, sometimes it grows and blossoms with more frequent contact
Feelings die	Feelings persist

Is the idea of a relationship lasting forever out of date? We all change over the years, so is it realistic to expect to stay with the same person for fifty years?

For lovers who thoroughly enjoy each other, there is no reason to ever let go. Would you give up your most prized possession? People who move on are not really involved. Because for years we have not fully understood the different kinds of love, and how essential high RAQ scores are, many relationships that should never have gotten going have contributed to the belief that love doesn't last. But true romantic chemistry does last. It can be turned off temporarily, but always has the capacity to resurface.

Back in 1929, Gilbert V. Hamilton did extensive research on the subject of love, and he found that among a group of college students he studied, there were an average of 6.7 romances per person. Yet only fifteen percent of these romances led to marriage. If both the partners shared strong romantic excitement, it would have been difficult for them to part. Lovers who are both strongly attracted to each other usually find ways to be together and stay together. So the students who didn't marry most likely thought they were in love when in actuality they were only infatuated.

In my practice I've seen infatuation last from the typical few weeks to several months, and on occasion, even a year or two. Infatuation is a false-positive indication of attraction and follows a predictable sequence.

Let's look at the male side of the story. As a child, a boy observes his mother's interaction with the man of the house and the world at large. He is very fond of his mother; she gives affection, food, security, attention, and approval. She solves problems; she heals injuries. But there are some things about her he doesn't like. She says no; she punishes; she makes him wait; she makes him eat food he doesn't like. And even though each mother is different, each son falls in love with his mother as a normal part of his growing up. He also knows sooner or later that even though he may want to marry her when he grows up, it is impossible. So he starts, almost subconsciously, to build up his fantasy of the woman he will be allowed to have as his very own. She will have all the positive traits of Mom, but none of the negative traits. As the boy gets older and meets women and things begin to click, he experiences a delight that accompanies the thought, "I've found you!" But as weeks or months go by, he discovers that the woman he has found is not who or what he thought she was or would be. As reality confronts him, he realizes it was infatuation, not love.

Infatuation is often a mental-emotional fantasy trip, sometimes promising triumph over the past. Genuine romantic chemistry may feel much the same as infatuation, but it is a biopsychological force and is a totally different phenomenon altogether. That these two vastly different things can in the beginning produce much the same feelings is a remarkable but true phenomenon.

Alan, a twenty-eight-year-old patient of mine, became involved with twenty-four-year-old Nansey and lived with her for a year in a semisatisfactory relationship. Four days before they were to be married, he called me in a state of panic. He had just called off the wedding; his bride-to-be was extremely upset; his family and friends thought he had lost his mind. Alan had suddenly realized that infatuation had got him started, habit had kept his relationship going, and social pressures were about to seal his fate. As difficult as calling off the wedding was, it was easier than a subsequent divorce would have been.

Should couples live together before getting married?
People who live together for six months to a year before marrying have a chance to really get to know each other. But this arrangement is not recommended for those couples who would be violating their moral, religious, or philosophical beliefs. It should also be remembered that, when living together in a de facto but not really committed marriage, the woman is typically in a more vulnerable position. There can be the temptation for the man to try to control the relationship by holding the promise of marriage or the threat of non-marriage over the head of his lover.

For couples who live together for two or three years or more, it is just as hard for them to terminate their relationship as it would be for people who have been married for that time.

Sex as a Special Kind of Infatuation

Dan, who came to see me when he was twenty-nine, said that he married while he was in college—he was twenty and his wife was nineteen. She was physically attractive; he was a virgin. When he met Peggy and they became physically involved, he thought he had found heaven. He was sure these wonderful feelings meant he was in love. In one sense he *was* in love, but he was in love with sex, not with Peggy. As an inexperienced youth, he could not know the difference.

Believing he was in love with Peggy, he married her and, for two years, everything seemed great. Peggy was in love with Dan in the sense of true romantic chemistry, and this was one of the reasons why their sexual relationship was so outstandingly satisfying. After their second year, Dan began to feel that something was missing. The sex was still excellent, but Dan could find no pleasurable involvement with his wife. He found himself looking forward only to their sex life together and nothing else. He thought he must have some kind of psychological problem and went for therapy. After seeing several therapists over a period of years, he ended up in my office.

When he filled out the Romantic Attraction Questionnaire, it became clear to him that the attraction to his wife was sexual only. His romantic attraction to her was very low.

Dan and Peggy's story is a common one. Many, many people confuse sex with true love. Sex attracts, but physical attraction alone cannot bind two people happily together for very long.

Sex is very intimate at the physical level, but there may not be much personal or emotional depth involved. The mysterious energy that we call romantic attraction is only partially related to sex, but it is this energy that is needed to sustain a lifetime of happiness together. Most people marry someone whom they find to be an interesting, exciting companion.

SEX OR TRUE ROMANTIC CHEMISTRY?
SIMILARITIES AND DIFFERENCES

Sex	True Romantic Chemistry
Similarities	
Very pleasurable	Very pleasurable
Differences	
A great many people can enjoy it with each other	Experienced with fewer people
Enjoy each other in a physical way	Enjoy each other in many different ways
Can be bored with partner when sex is over	Continued interest in partner after sex
Variable to weak interest in permanent relationship	Very strong desire for permanent relationship
Focus of enjoyment is physical	Focus of enjoyment is in the other person's personality
May or may not include true romantic chemistry	Almost always includes strong sexual interest and satisfaction
May or may not be a strong interest in the other person's pleasure and well-being	There is a strong interest in the other person's pleasure and well-being
Relationship may end quickly when difficulties arise	Strong interest in continuing relationship despite difficulties
Desire is for physical pleasure	Desire is for lifelong relationship
Provides a temporary sense of well-being	Provides a lasting feeling of belonging
There may or may not be a strong protective interest toward the partner	There is a strong protective interest toward the partner

Long-Distance Romance

I'm not a great believer in long-distance romances, because they can prolong the infatuation stage.

If a couple can't see each other as frequently as three or four times a week, the infatuation period will be extended. Since long-distance romances can go on for long periods of time, they are often surviving the fantasy of infatuation. I've even counseled a case of infatuation that lasted for almost two years because the couple saw each other only once a week.

Long-distance lovers have insufficient contact with each other to really know each other. They idealize each other, they believe that their lives will be better when they are united, and they attribute assumed rather than real powers to their long-distance lovers.

Meanwhile, they are living in a world of fantasy, taken in by their imaginations and believing they have a solid relationship. Some long-distance romances work out. Many more do not.

Tim was a doctor and Karen a nurse when they fell in love—or thought they fell in love. Very soon after they met, Tim was awarded a fellowship at a hospital two thousand miles away. Karen couldn't find a job in that city, and since the fellowship was just for a year, they felt they could commute on weekends and holidays. Tim's schedule was so difficult that he didn't see Karen for three months after the move, but he thought about her constantly. When they finally did get together, Tim found Karen "different." While they were apart, Tim had fantasized Karen into being something she wasn't. When they were together, Tim was no longer content with the "real" Karen, he preferred his fantasy vision. They broke up shortly thereafter.

The Test of Time

If your relationship is as good six months later as it was the day you met, you probably have the basis of a long-term relationship.

In my practice I've seen that it's easy for people to get involved with each other, easy to move in with a lover, and hard, very hard, to break up and move out.

Romantic attraction does not wane over time. When you have the real thing, nothing can or will make it go away. Unhappy experiences or frustration or disappointment can squeeze romantic attraction down for a period of time, but romantic attraction can always be restored with careful attention.

Before you marry or move in with your lover, let your relationship stand the test of time. It is wise to spend three to six months getting to know each other before you make any important decisions.

I had a love affair with a man when I was in college. Although we wanted to marry, I decided not to marry the first man who asked me, realizing that there was a lot more of the world, and men, to know. That was ten years ago, and I've never found anyone as wonderful as my first lover. He was gold and I didn't know it. Is there any going back?

This has happened to a lot of people, and many are sadder but wiser. A few actually manage to recontact their old lovers to see if there is a future for them.

What's required of young people is very paradoxical; they're asked to make career commitments and romantic commitments when they have very little to go on. They don't know for sure what they really want or who they really are. So they may let a lover go and, later, regret their decision bitterly.

Some actually do manage to get reunited. Sometimes it works out and sometimes it doesn't. It does work when there was real mutual romantic chemistry. When it doesn't, the relationship entailed some element of infatuation. The relationship didn't go on long enough for it to collapse of its own weight, so there is a fantasy element that may last indefinitely, even a lifetime. "Oh, gee, if I could only go back to John or Mary." If it was infatuation, and John and Mary are reunited, the bubble will probably burst very quickly. A lot of that goes on. People frequently fantasize about "the one that got away."

Fantasy or Reality?

With infatuation, you falsely believe that you are genuinely romantically in love. You *think* that chemistry is there until you learn that it is not. With the fantasy lovemate, one lover is mistaken in his knowledge about how his partner truly feels. And while there may be difficult spots in the marriage, the person who is fantasizing sees past these times of troubles to a day when things will become better. Part of the fantasy is that things will indeed become better, sooner or later.

"Things will be better when Ted is out of medical school."

"Things will be better when the kids are in school and out of diapers."

"Things will be better when we get out of financial straits."

"Things will be better when we move to a new town."

Things will probably not get better.

But for the person in love, living with fantasy often feels safer and is more comforting than living with the truth. It is difficult, sometimes impossible, for the person in love to see and accept reality. Reality is painful. Reality is rude. Reality may mean divorce.

That's because the person who stays in the fantasy world has a high degree of romantic attraction for his partner. He *wants* to believe that everything really will work out, that romance really is mutual.

It takes considerable maturity and strength to face

the truth, but the truth is that the other partner just might not share such a high degree of romantic attraction.

The Story of Stan, an Innocent, Tragic Mistake

Stan was my patient eighteen years ago. In those days I was a somewhat traditional psychologist dealing with the problems of people in traditional ways. When Stan came to me, I was certain he had a curable neurosis and after intensive therapy he would go on to a happier, richer, and fuller life. Little did I know that Stan would change my life and the entire way in which I would conduct my practice.

Stan came to me during seven years of intermittent therapy as his life was being torn apart. I searched in vain for neurosis as I listened to his descriptions of his childhood, his parents, his dreams, and his fears. But his only problems were related to his love life.

Stan and Michelle had been married for fifteen years and had three lovely children. Then Stan met Kimberly. He had never had an extra-marital affair and wasn't looking for one now. But when he met Kim, something explosive happened to both of them. He thought he was happily married; he believed he loved Michelle; but he couldn't get Kim and their relationship out of his mind.

Kim divorced her husband immediately. Stan came to me for help. For six years he battled his conscience while he kept up a clandestine affair with Kim.

The more I worked with Stan, the more frustrated I became. He was not neurotic. He was not suffering from an unresolved Oedipus complex, nor was he acting out a scenario from childhood that he was forced to futilely replay for the rest of his life. Stan was just a nice average guy, who happened to be caught in a life dilemma.

Then, after enduring more than six years of Stan's

vacillating over which one of these two ladies was to be his one and only life partner, Kim announced that it was all over.

"You're never going to marry me. I love you, but you won't leave your wife and I can't take this anymore," she cried. "I've found another boyfriend, and if he wants to marry me, then I'm going to marry him. I've got to think of my future. I'll never love anyone like I love you, but I can't take this anymore."

Stan went berserk. He knew he couldn't live without Kim. He rushed over to her apartment, literally kicked out her new boyfriend, and vowed to resolve his marital problems the next day.

Michelle was quite shocked to learn that her husband had been having an affair for over six years. She knew their marriage wasn't perfect, but she was satisfied with it. She assumed that Stan loved her as much as she loved him and thought he was just having a mid-life crisis and would soon regain his senses.

Stan and Michelle came in together for therapy. If I had developed The Love Test materials then, we would have known the answer to their problems immediately. Michelle would have probably rated her romantic attraction toward Stan as very high, but Stan would have probably rated his feelings for Michelle as only lukewarm at best. Stan and Kimberly, on the other hand, would have scored their feelings for each other as very high. Stan just didn't have enough romantic attraction for Michelle. Since he had *never* felt a greater attraction toward someone else, he did not know that other feelings existed. Then he met Kim. He was transformed and delighted by true love and confused and enmeshed in a very serious ethical conflict.

"If I had known the kind of feelings I have for Kim were even possible, I never would have married my wife," he sadly admitted.

Stan and Michelle eventually divorced; he and Kim married and are living together today, happily. Michelle went for therapy to deal with her tragic rejection and to start a new life. If Michelle and Stan could have used The Love Test, they never would have married and faced the traumas they endured.

So there we were. Stan had spent a lot of money. I had spent a lot of time and energy with Stan and his life crisis. I knew he didn't have a neurosis. I learned that having the wrong love partner can make you think you have a neurosis. And I saw how Stan's problems were solved when he and Kim decided to get married.

Life with the right partner is better on all levels.

Stan and I both discovered this at the same time.

I began to see my other patients from Stan's point of view. It soon became clear to me that only about half of them had neuroses. The others were merely living with or married to the wrong person.

I decided that Freud had missed one very big boat.

Many people *do* have neurotic problems. But many people undergoing therapy have no neurosis whatsoever and are mistaken to believe they do. They can and will live happier ever after once they find the partner who is right for them.

He Loves Me, He Loves Me Not

How your partner treats you is a direct function of his degree of romantic attraction to you and his own emotional maturity.

Caring treatment should be the reward of any serious relationship. People who are involved in fantasy relationships often delude themselves into thinking that there really isn't anything wrong with their love affair or their marriage, that things will indeed get better, someday. When they are unhappy or upset, they remind themselves that they have nothing concrete to complain about. The treatment they may be getting from their spouses or lovers isn't what they want, but materially they are well taken care of. They tell themselves that they could be in worse shape, and then they try to count their blessings.

The material benefits are usually clear: a co[...] home, a second car, membership in the cou[...] and camp for the kids, a night out for dinner [...] movies, and an annual summer vacation. What could be wrong?

They are not being emotionally well taken care of.

When you are emotionally well taken care of, you get the kind of caring treatment from your lover or spouse that you desire and deserve. This treatment has little to do with being well taken care of materially or financially. Only romantic attraction and emotional maturity motivate a person to give as much personal attention as necessary for a mutually fulfilling relationship.

If Mom told you that the love you give out will inevitably come back to you, she was either unfortunately wrong or the happy partner in a special love relationship.

The treatment you give someone and the treatment you get too often have little correlation. This doesn't mean your partner is an unfeeling, callow person. It simply means he or she doesn't have the romantic attraction and/or the emotional maturity to come through for you. This very same person who is not interested in you may come through with flowers and poetry for someone else.

Leah and Max were expectant parents out shopping for a layette when they happened to bump into Janey, Max's ex-wife. Leah excitedly told Janey all about the baby's new room and the things that Max had done for the baby: painting walls, building a cradle from scratch, and even a catcher's mitt waiting for the expected son.

Janey kept shaking her head in disbelief.

"I don't believe this is the same man I knew," she kept muttering.

When Janey was pregnant with her and Max's child, she couldn't get his attention at all. He worked late, refused to attend natural childbirth classes, and grew bored when she talked about their expected baby. They divorced when the baby was a year old.

Max was not a changed person, but the difference in his romantic attraction for Leah compared to his feel-ngs for Janey was immense. And that's why Leah was receiving caring treatment from Max and why Janey would always wonder at the changes in her husband. The changed behavior was motivated by romantic interest. With enough emotional maturity it will continue.

Sex and the Proper Partner

Caring treatment extends from all other aspects of your life-style, including the bedroom. You don't have to be in love with the person with whom you have sex. But there is a tremendous difference in the kind of sex you can have with a romantically turned on and emotionally mature partner.

Very few lasting relationships are made in bed. Fantasies may begin and end there; true love does not. Relationships based on a strong degree of romantic attraction do lead to good sex. And the sex rarely fades or dies out. The frequency of sexual activity may lessen as the years go by, but the satisfaction remains high or even improves. The honeymoon is never over, the bloom never off the rose.

Can lovemaking really be as good after several years as it was in the beginning?

Lovemaking as a term has two different meanings. When it is used as a polite term for sex, it is still just sex. But when lovemaking also means genuine, mutual caring, the joining together of two people with affection, personal expressions of endearment and appreciation, and a delight in the wonder that is another person's personality, lovemaking will continue to satisfy and will probably improve.

Most romantically involved couples who are reasonably mature report richer and more rewarding lovemaking that deepens as time goes by. Masters and Johnson's research shows that sexual satisfaction goes on into their eighties for those couples who remain sexually active.

Dr. William Appleton, a Harvard Medical School psychiatrist, researched the frequency of sexual intimacy of couples who said their marriages were working. Two percent never had sex; eight percent had sex less than once a month; twenty-three percent had sex on the average of 2.3 times a month; twenty-four percent had sex once weekly; thirty-one percent had sex two or three times weekly; twelve percent had sex 4.5 times a week; and only one percent had sex daily. Yet each couple reported that the marriage was working and that the "emotional context" of the marriage was more important than the frequency of sex. Sex is very nice, but it's not all there is to a good relationship.

Can you be in love without having a hot and heavy sexual relationship?

Definitely yes. There are great variations among people in terms of sex drive or interest. If two people have a genuinely low sex drive, they can be very happy with each other because they like, trust, and respect each other. In fact, the companionship factor is typically the biggest factor in most relationships.

On the average, a thirty-five-year-old couple are probably spending two to three evenings a week making love, usually for about a half hour. The typical time for lovemaking is a few hours a week, but there can be as many as ten or twenty hours a week spent discussing issues and sharing experiences. Usually the most satisfying and most frequent lovemaking is found in those relationships characterized by emotional maturity and romantic attraction, one reason being that distancing games are not played with sex as a gambit.

If your sex life is suffering, it may well be one of the first clues to a problem of one-way romance in your relationship. The romantically excited partner usually feels that the sex is great, but the partner who is not romantically excited will feel that something is missing. Improved sexual technique usually will not help, because what is missing is a sufficient degree of romantic interest.

With infatuation, the sex starts out great and dwindles as the realities of life set in. Sex with the wrong partner is only sex.

Sex between the right partners is fulfilling. And if there is a sexual problem between two right-for-each-other partners, invariably some sexual counseling will bring about significant improvement.

A great many people go through life having sexual affairs—confusing love and sex and wondering why they never win at love. Yet there is no need to be confused. There is a difference between sex, infatuation, and true romantic attraction.

Should This Marriage Be Saved?

Many marriages can and should be saved. However, just as many cannot and should not be.

Unfortunately, a large proportion of couples—approximately half—should never have married their present partners! They never should have been dating seriously or living together in an attempt to make it as a couple. They may be very nice people, but they just weren't meant for each other.

Divorce is the best thing that could happen to many of them, and to their families. Once the unfortunate separate, each partner has a chance of finding the right person for him or her and discovering the joys of lasting love. Even children of such marriages will be better off when their parents stop squabbling and find partners who are better suited to them.

So don't try to save a marriage that can't be saved. It is my firm belief that the main cause of divorce is marrying a partner who is wrong *for you*.

Some marriage counselors may advise you differently. If it's the marriage counselor's job to "save" any kind of marriage, his success may be judged by whether or not a couple stays together. If a marriage counselor advises you to stay together for another year or two or even five years, is he a "good" counselor? Why should you invest another five years in a mistake? That's what I call misguided advice. Don't let an old-fashioned view of divorce or a lack of confidence in your own ability keep you tied in a hopeless relationship.

You deserve the best possible relationship you can find and develop. I do not contend that counseling or therapy is a waste of time. They are invaluable keys to improving emotional maturity. But I feel very strongly that if you use the materials offered in The Love Test, you will have a good idea of the strengths and weaknesses of your personal relationship. Therapy designed to save a marriage usually is futile when there is *only one* person who has a strong romantic interest. No amount of therapy can change romantic interest. Counseling, however, can always help those who have a problem with immaturity, if the immature person is sufficiently motivated to get help. In a one-way romance, a new partner is probably called for. Your first step should be to get the most accurate possible diagnosis of the strong and weak points in your relationship.

How big a factor should your children be in the decision to get a divorce?
Very big, but they are seldom the main factor in making this decision. The two main factors are romantic interest that goes only one way and one partner with an immaturity problem who will not go for counseling.

As for children, young ones are initially very disturbed about divorce and feel that the world is falling apart; however, as soon as regular visitation is established, their fears and insecurities rapidly diminish. Children often blame their bad behavior for the divorce. They come to this false conclusion because they are so self-centered that they tend to see their own behavior as the cause of bad effects. Children should be prepared in advance of a breakup, instead of having it suddenly

COMPARISON OF SEX, INFATUATION, ROMANTIC ATTRACTION, AND EMOTIONAL MATURITY

Sex	Infatuation	Romantic Attraction	Emotional Maturity
Biological urge	Wish-fulfillment, fantasy trip that ends as reality impacts, showing the fantasy to be a false indicator of true romantic attraction; the false belief is that the romantic partner has been found	A biopsychological attraction to another person's personality, a sense of pleasurable excitement, desire for intimate association, and the desire to be very much desired by the other person	The degree to which a person has developed coping ability in terms of having insight into one's self, to relate constructively in social relationships, to be able to solve life's problems, to have self-discipline, and to behave with high ethical standards.
Gives temporary satisfaction	Gives temporary thrill of having found an exciting and fulfilling companion	Gives very long-term satisfaction when the attraction and pleasure are mutual	Gives steadily increasing ability to cope realistically and effectively with the demands and challenges of life. Embodies the capacity to treat another person with respect and dignity and

Interest can be one way or mutual	Can be one way or mutual, but always ends, usually quite soon	Can be one way or mutual. Once beyond the infatuation period, it typically lasts a lifetime. If it is there, we don't know how to make it go away. If it isn't there, we don't know how to bring it about.	caring. Brings out the best in other people.
			Anyone who wishes can become more mature by practicing more mature behavior. Everyone can grow up emotionally, if the desire, determination, and efforts are strong enough.
Can be very boring if not accompanied by romantic attraction	Sequence is pleasure, followed by disappointment, disinterest	There is, when mutual, great satisfaction, fulfillment, with sex, companionship. When not mutual, is very frustrating, difficult to be together.	When present, builds strong relationships; when absent, destroys relationships, even if there is strong romantic interest
Purpose: procreation, via pleasure	Purpose: the wish to have found the lover	Can hold two people together forever, if enough maturity is present	Assures successful adjustment to life.

ounced. This will reduce the sense of shock and the rt feelings of having been excluded or rejected.

Some people decide to stay together until the kids are grown, but this trend is disappearing as more and more adults want to live now and not postpone their own personal happiness.

A Changing View of Divorce

Both partners enter into marriage with high hopes and the best intentions. Each partner assumes an equal share of the responsibility for the decision to marry. If they separate, therefore, there should be no judgments, no blame.

Preventing divorce by marrying the right partner for you in the first place is the best of all possible plans. Staying unhappily together in order to prevent a divorce is an evasion of your problems. Some people equate divorce with failure and think that if they end their marriage, they will be labeled "losers." By remaining unhappily married, they hang on to the hope that if they can't be winners, at least they won't seem to be losers.

You are not a failure if you get divorced. You are only a failure if you keep repeating the same mistakes.

According to the exams we took in this book, my husband and I should split up. The fire may be gone, but we're not unhappy together. We're used to our life-style the way it is; are you sure the test works?

The test materials have been developed over the past ten years with hundreds of patients and thousands of students. With all these people, these tests have had a better than ninety percent accuracy rate for assessing the strengths and weaknesses of a relationship and predicting future happiness.

The well-trained clinical psychologist understands how to use tests and measurements, how to read and analyze statistics, and how to judge bias and subjectivity.

Moreover, he or she is capable of constructing an instrument to measure a wide range of human knowledge, sentiment, and behavior. The Love Test materials were developed with consideration to all these factors.

Your experience of the "fire" being gone, and being used to life the way it is, is a very common one. Initial excitement about new things in our lives is usually followed by a somewhat lesser degree of excitement. However, what usually happens in our love relationships is that we tend to take each other for granted, not realizing that a continuing daily display of warm personal interest is like periodically adding a fresh log to a fire; it keeps it alive and glowing. Anything, including our relationships, tends to degrade if not looked after. By assuming that we are getting all that is possible from each other, we create a self-fulfilling prophecy. While enjoying the comfortable security you have with each other, you can bring back more of that fire that you may unfortunately believe is "gone."

If the results of your scores on the exams in this book do not jibe with your own personal experiences, please retest. Usually in cases like this, someone has not understood the directions. However, no test is perfect. If you are thinking about a very major decision, why not invest a few hundred dollars and take your test results for a professional opinion? No one should split up without having counseling first. Do not split up just because of information you read in this book. That would be one more example of divorcing for the wrong reasons.

Changing partners doesn't automatically guarantee success or happiness the next time around. You will only have the lasting love you seek when both your romantic attraction and emotional maturity are mutually and sufficiently high. If the partners in a couple do not share reasonably high romantic attraction for each other, there's good reason to think they might separate.

On the other hand, if both partners have a high degree of romantic attraction and they are considering divorce, chances are they are separating for the wrong reasons and that counseling really *can* help. You can be very much in love and have a maturity problem that can be solved. With help, you can enjoy the love match you have already made.

In such a case, it's not very likely that you will find a happier relationship with someone else, so you might as well get help. If one of you (or both of you, for that matter) in this situation refuses to get help, then and only then is a separation advocated. Things don't get better on their own. Working at upgrading your marriage will bring you the happier love life you desire—and deserve.

Chapter Two

♡ ♡ ♡

Romantic
Attraction

"When I first met him, it hit me like a bolt of lightning; he had a magnetic personality. His very presence filled the room. I knew I would never forget him."

"There was a glow to her that drew me to her. Something special buzzed in the air around her, and I didn't know what it was except that I liked it. Every time I was around her there was a feeling of excitement; when I wasn't with her, I was thinking about her. She was constantly on my mind."

What is this magnetic force? This excitement? This inexplicable energy that draws two people together and leaves them convinced that they were made for each other and that there is no one else in the world quite as perfect for them?

Some call it love; some call it neurosis. I call it *romantic attraction*.

It's an invisible energy that may or may not be mutual and strikes without reason. Romantic attraction knows no age boundaries; it never discriminates; it may be pleasurable or painful depending on the other circumstances that surround its bite. The power of romantic attraction cannot be harnessed or altered by those who experience it.

Romantic attraction is different from infatuation or sex; it is also different from the feelings we have when we like, trust, and respect another person. Affection and sex are two facets of romantic attraction, but they are only part of its realm. Romantic attraction is the sense of excitement that you experience about another person, that indefinable, powerful desire to associate with him or her in a very intimate way, a desire to be special and valuable in that person's life. Romantic attraction encompasses the desire for belonging, companionship, intimacy, and deep affection. When you feel a high degree of romantic attraction for another person, you want to be with that person as often as possible. You want him or her to *want* you! The time you are apart can be agony for you. When you are not together, life is less pleasant. You feel lonely until you are reunited with your lover. This is the person you choose not only to sleep with, but also to wake up with, to go places with, to be your date on New Year's Eve, to be your partner in many things, big and small.

Are women more interested in love than men?

No. That is a myth in our culture that Lord Byron fostered when he wrote, "Man's love is of man's life a thing apart,/'Tis woman's whole existence." The belief was that women wanted love and men wanted sex, but that's wrong, all wrong. Men want love every bit as much as women do, and they want both kinds of love—romance and caring.

In strong mutual romantic attraction, there is a shared sense of excitement in each other's companionship and affection. The chemistry feels right and good. Something very special is happening. Sometimes it is described as "the two of us are one." This delightful closeness gives the feeling of a shared psyche.

Romantic attraction is like an electrical spark that sets a friendship on fire. When accompanied by high emotional maturity, it is a caring, quiet understanding, a

mutual confidence, a sharing and forgiving. It is lo
through good times and bad; it settles for less t
perfection and makes allowance for human weakness

Romantic attraction refers to the degree of pleasurable excitement that one person feels toward another
person, the degree of interest in getting to know someone better, in associating intimately. It is experienced as
the desire to spend time with another person, to be
included in his or her world, to be wholeheartedly and
unconditionally accepted by that person. To have the
other person's deep and affectionate interest is as paramount as to be respected, appreciated, and admired.

As we've already seen, romantic interest cannot be
differentiated from infatuation in the early stages of a
relationship. The feelings of pleasurable excitement are
the same, but infatuation usually collapses within the
first few months of a new relationship. True romantic
interest is most likely a deep, biopsychological response.
It very often occurs on the first meeting. But so does
infatuation, so be careful.

Romantic Energy, Invisible but Powerful

When you are romantically excited about someone, you
feel that something very unusual and special is happening.
You get a thrill when you think about that person. Life
feels better. You feel lucky to know that person and you
want to be with him or her. You enjoy talking to that
person. You look forward to sharing affection and sex.
You have a strong urge to hold that person in your arms
and sometimes feel you never want to let go. You want
to keep that person forever. You want to take him or her
along with you and share your life experiences. You
want to do more things together than there is time for.
And most of all, you want very much for that person to
want you.

You look forward to signs of interest and approval,
and are frightened and worried about possibly losing
them. You can feel insecure and jealous. You can be-

come anxious or worried about the possibility of displeasing that person, because you can't be happy when that person is unhappy with you. You feel a strong urge for total and permanent commitment. You feel terribly vulnerable. You *are* terribly vulnerable.

Romantic Attraction Means Being Vulnerable

There is no such thing as being in love without being vulnerable. When we are very romantically attracted to someone, we are wide open to all those "slings and arrows." Our heightened desire to spend time with that person, to be included in his or her world, to be wholeheartedly and unconditionally accepted by that person makes us painfully sensitive to any form of rejection. From that person, the slightest criticism or ridicule carries damning weight.

Because we spend so much time with our partner, we become susceptible to all the disappointments and frustrations of living intimately with another person. We must accommodate our partner's failures and inadequacies. We must put up with our partner's illnesses, idiosyncracies, moods, and fears, just as our partner must tolerate our foibles and failures.

This vulnerability tends to make us overreact and misinterpret our lover's actions. We may interpret an appointment's not being kept as a sign of dwindling affection rather than as indication of car trouble. We may even torment ourselves with visions of possible long separation, or even the death of our love. But the rejection lovers probably fear most is hearing the partner in their love relationship say, "The thrill is gone." Or, "I've found someone else." Those words can be the death knell not only for the love relationship but sometimes for our self-confidence as well.

Are You a Romantic Virgin?

Jenny is twenty-five and has had several "relationships," but she has never experienced the kind of strong romantic attraction that lasts more than a month. She's had half a dozen infatuations and now she has begun to doubt this thing called "falling in love" or "being head over heels in love." Her view is that it's "always infatuation" and that people who believe in romantic love just haven't gotten over their infatuation yet. She grows more and more cynical daily. In fact, she's considering marrying Gary, who's been after her for some time. They've been dating for two years, they've seen a lot of each other, and there is true romantic chemistry on his part. Jenny likes, respects, and trusts Gary. He's a very nice man and she knows he'd be a good husband. But she just can't feel the same excitement for him that he feels for her. She is not suffering from a fear problem. She simply has never known a man with whom she got beyond the infatuation state.

Jenny is a romantic virgin.

I see her as a land mine that could go off at any time. Someday, somewhere, somehow, she's going to meet a man with whom she feels a high degree of romantic chemistry. Love can strike anyone at any time! And after being married to Gary for a few years, and mothering a child or two, she could wind up exploding her marriage and her family relationship.

Romantic virgins operate out of a lack of experience. They are not willingly deceiving themselves or their lovers. They marry someone not knowing that more powerful feelings exist. Romantic virgins just haven't met the right person yet. They have never experienced true romantic attraction.

Romantic virgins make mistaken matches or marriages because they are as innocent as virgins. They just don't know any better. Later, if they meet a person they are truly romantically attracted to, they will say, "I just didn't know these kinds of feelings existed." Only then will the "mistake" be realized. The best thing a romantic virgin can do is to wait and watch. One of my patients said, "I've heard that you have to kiss a lot of frogs before you find the one who turns into a prince."

One-Way Romance Is Not Rejection

Self-doubt exists in all of us, and the less self-confident we are, the more doubts we have. Using the RAQ can show if your doubts about your feelings toward your love partner are well founded.

It is very common to suffer from one-way love. It's what the songbirds call unrequited love, and is evident whenever one person rates another with a high score on the RAQ but the degree of romantic attraction is not shared by the other partner. One-way interest happens all the time; it's a matter of luck, not a measure of your worth as a person.

A relationship with one-way romance is usually a doomed one. Someday your lover could find someone else to whom he or she is highly attracted. This is what happened to Stan (see pp. 16–18), who was also a romantic virgin. Your lover may then leave you, have an affair, or go through the agony of trying to solve a not very easily solved problem. One-way romance seldom leads to a fulfilling relationship.

That Feeling That Something Is Missing

Charlotte, who is forty-three, came to me with a complaint. "I just don't know what it is, but something has been missing all along. We've been married for twenty-two years, we have three wonderful children, but something is missing. Don't misunderstand. My husband, John, is a wonderful person. He's the exact opposite of my father, who was so domineering I couldn't stand him. John is kind and flexible and easy to get along with—a terrific guy. But I'm telling you, something is missing. I've wondered if it was something wrong with me or him, then a friend who had taken your class told me to talk to you."

Charlotte filled out the Romantic Attraction Questionnaire and scored John at 137, much less than lukewarm interest. How could this marriage have gone on for twenty-two years?

Over a period of two months of sessions, it became increasingly clear that Charlotte was not now, nor had she ever been, romantically interested in her husband. What attracted her to him all those years ago was safety, ego, and security. "I wanted security, and he was very good-looking. I was attracted to his easygoing nature. He's a very nice person. I realize now that he was more enamored of me than I was of him, and that was flattering to my ego."

The something that was missing was romantic excitement.

Should you never marry until you find a person whose RAQ matches your own?

No. It's not a matter of matching. Rather, it's a matter of both partners scoring 220 or above on the RAQ and also having good scores on the EMRF. When they have RAQ scores of over 220, they get the assurance that things are going to go well in their marriage, provided each partner is emotionally mature. Also, it's better when the man is at least a little more interested than the woman. That tends to make up for the power differential that exists in today's culture. Fair or not, men still have more power than women.

If a man's RAQ score is somewhat higher than a woman's score then his interest in her is stronger, and he is therefore *more highly motivated* to please her. This "advantage" that the woman has can be thought of as compensating for society's generally granting more power to men. If the woman's RAQ is higher than the man's, her coming on to him with a stronger interest, because of his luck to be a male, then gives him a double "advantage" in the relationship. These power factors can be very important when it comes time to resolve basic conflicts and come up with a solution that is reasonably fair to both.

Sex and Romantic Attraction

As we've already seen, sex is different from romantic attraction (see pp. 6–8), but sex is a factor in romantic attraction. Being cared about, being touched, and being loved are all important aspects of the affection that is bountiful when romantic attraction is high. This affection automatically culminates in sex, but it is sex as an expression of affection. You can have sex with just about anyone, but sex with a stranger is a biological function that typically has little to do with true love.

It is not uncommon for a woman to come to me for help because she is anorgasmic; that is, she has never experienced an orgasm. She has read enough magazine articles, seen enough movies, and talked to her friends enough to know she is missing something and would like to do something about it. Take the case of Jaye.

Jaye was twenty-two when she married Steve. Her sexual experience prior to meeting Steve was limited and she had never truly been in love with anyone. Steve was eight years older, well established as the head of his own company, and came across as the winner he was. He was tall, handsome, had sparkling blue eyes, and spoke very rapidly because he had such enthusiasm for life. Jaye, like everyone else who met Steve, was really impressed by him. When he asked her to marry him, she hesitated only briefly before saying yes. She knew she wasn't really in love with Steve, but she knew what a good "catch" he was, and that he would be a devoted husband. Jaye had no serious career plans, felt pressured by her peers to be doing something with her life, and saw being married to Steve as a way out of having to perform in a job she believed she might not be able to keep. Steve was her white knight who swooped down and rescued her from reality.

After six years of marriage, Jaye came to me worried about the fact she had never had an orgasm, tearfully admitting that all this time she had been "faking it." Steve, of course, knew nothing of her problem. Jaye had already tried a number of sex books and had recently bought a vibrator.

After hearing her story, I gave Jaye the Romantic Attraction Questionnaire, on which she rated her romantic feelings for Steve. She rated her feelings at only 160. Low romantic attraction often is a reason for a woman being anorgasmic. She really wasn't very attracted to her husband. No matter how high he would have rated his feelings for her on the same test, and I'm sure he would have rated them in the high 200's, Jaye would have remained sexually dissatisfied and confused because she was not romantically excited about Steve. She had married her husband for all the wrong reasons and, while she thought she was happily married, the truth was quickly revealed in her RAQ. Women like Jaye, when in bed with a man they are very romantically excited about (rating anywhere from 225 to 300 on the Romantic Attraction Questionnaire), will often have their first orgasm if not right away, then soon after.

I mention the case of Jaye to point out two important things. First, sexual dysfunction when related to psychological functions (that means there's nothing biologically wrong) could very well be related to romantic feelings about a sex partner. And second, just as we have discovered that people who are happy in love are happy in life, it is true that people who are *really* in love, true love, usually have good sexual relationships.

How important is physical attraction?

Very important. Physical appearance is probably the first element that attracts us to another person (even of the same sex). Research shows that physically attractive people have more invitations to get acquainted. But what attracts is not necessarily what holds. There is no research that I know of that shows that physically attractive people have happier love lives. Physical attraction compared to true romantic chemistry is probably best described as "you can't judge a book by its cover." However, we don't usually get to know another person unless he or she has at least marginal physical attraction *for us*.

I'm not a homosexual, but I have very satisfying relationships with my friends and don't feel that being married for the sake of being married is that important. My mother is very worried about it. Is there something wrong with me?

Not at all. The mature person realizes there's a lot involved in being happily married and that being married for the sake of being married has no meaningful purpose. The other point is that excitement doesn't only apply to relationships with members of the opposite sex. You can have a good friend you thoroughly enjoy; you can have a nephew, an aunt, a grandparent, a neighbor, or a business associate with whom you enjoy spending time. The excitement factor is what's important.

You can also be romantically excited about a thing rather than a person. Lewis and Clark were romantically excited about the Northwest; Thomas Edison was romantically excited about his laboratory. This isn't romance in the everyday sense of the word, but it's adventure, excitement, or passion just the same. And passion about any kind of constructive pursuit can make life more fulfilling.

Mutual Romantic Attraction: Important, but Not Everything

On its own, the Romantic Attraction Questionnaire is a very useful diagnostic tool. What it measures is an energy that attracts, an energy that cannot be manufactured. If your Romantic Attraction Questionnaire score indicates that "it just isn't there" for you, nothing I know can stimulate the kind of depth of feeling I am talking about and calling true romantic attraction. A couple may compare their RAQ scores and immediately see why the course of true love has seemed rather lopsided and unbalanced. One-way love is a serious problem for which there is no real cure.

It's not an easy thing to have your worst fears confirmed for you on a piece of paper. But you need to know that there are many couples who do not share extremely high romantic attraction, yet who are living comfortably together.

Is it true that, in a love relationship, one person loves more than the other person?

That is often the case, although I have seen many couples whose RAQ scores are within five points of each other's. But it's hard to find a couple where both partners have identical RAQ scores and identical emotional maturity profiles.

If your RAQ score is higher than your partner's, then you love him or her more in the romantic sense. If his or her emotional maturity has fewer weaknesses than yours, then, as far as mature love goes, your partner is more loving than you are. Remember that love, in the complete sense of the word, is a *combination* of romantic attraction and emotional maturity.

If there is a power differential in your relationship, it's quite possible that the more powerful person is the one who rates his or her partner with the lower RAQ.

Keep in mind that RAQ ratings need not be identical to be high enough for a good love match. If Maria rates her feelings for Jules at 227 and Jules rates his feelings for Maria at 291, they still have a very good match.

Borderline Romantic Attraction

The maximum score on the Romantic Attraction Questionnaire is 300. I've had a few people score 290 or above and have seen numerous scores in the 280 range. But I don't consider a case to be borderline until the score is between 200 and 220. If you have a borderline score, it may explain many feelings of confusion and uncertainty. You are probably listening to two voices in your head. One voice tells you something is missing and unsettles your psyche just enough for you to admit that you are nervous. The other voice tries to calm you down, tells you you're being ridiculous, that everything is just fine, that you shouldn't go looking for trouble, and that things could be a lot worse if you don't leave well enough alone. If you look at your score on the RAQ and find it falls between 200 and 220, use this information to gain another insight and a better understanding of why you have had such mixed emotions.

In borderline cases, you should be very careful not to make snap decisions. Don't draw any conclusions from your RAQ scores alone without the Emotional Maturity Rating Form scores and, even then, make sure you and your partner rerate. A divorce or separation is not necessarily called for in borderline cases. I've had many, many borderline cases where I've recommended to the patients or students that they stay married or proceed with marriage plans, making improvements in their personal maturity and developing a better attitude of appreciation for the benefits they do have in their relationship.

Jacqueline was thirty-two when she came to see me. She had moved to Southern California two years before after living ten years in Boston. The main reason she had left Boston was the breakup of her intense relationship with Nick, an academic and writer who was brilliant, high-strung and often very negative. He expected Jacqueline to pay the rent when he was low on funds, to cook for him, to clean and care for their apartment, and entertain his cadre of friends, with whom he had hung around since his undergraduate days.

Nick was moody, often rude, and unable to consider Jacqueline's feelings in any matter that should have called for a joint decision. Despite all this, Jacqueline

was crazy about Nick. When he refused to
counseling, Jacquie decided to move to Califor
came to me six months after her move. I had he
the Romantic Attraction Questionnaire, and she rated
her romantic attraction to Nick at 275. But Jacqueline
was sensible enough to know that as much as she loved
Nick, she was also miserable with him. She often said
she neither liked, respected, nor trusted him. The
price paid for the romantic interest was very high.

After a year in California, Jacqueline met Ben. Ben
didn't light her fire nearly as much as Nick had. In fact,
she rated her feelings for him at 210 on the Romantic
Attraction Questionnaire. Ben rated his feelings for
Jacqueline at 274. Both had a high degree of emotional
maturity. Jacqueline's questions to me came from the
depths of her soul. Was it a mistake to marry Ben?
Didn't she really still belong to Nick, heart and soul?
Should she go back to Boston and try to make things
work out? Could she be happy with Ben for the rest of
her life, or would she later regret the decision to marry
him and leave him or seek a divorce?

This is the problem with borderline cases. You don't
always know which trade-off will be the best. With
Jacqueline, we were able to steer toward a wise decision when she gave me more information about Ben.
She said she liked, trusted, and respected Ben, the
very opposite of her feelings for Nick, and that she very
much appreciated the way he treated her. And when I
heard that piece of information, I immediately reminded
Jacqueline of Bessell's primary law: *Caring treatment is
essential*. How someone treats you is the single most
important feature of your relationship, just a shade
more important than romantic interest, if you must
choose between the two. Unless you are a masochist,
you should be teamed with a partner who treats you the
way you want, and like, being treated.

When I heard these mature aspects of Ben's personality and character, I knew that Jacqueline and Ben had a
very good chance. Borderline scores on the RAQ probably mean that some therapy or even a few sessions of

professional advice can help in evaluating the trade-offs and coming to the most sensible decision. It's important to remember that romantic excitement is great, but there is also the consideration of how well you will be treated by your partner. Always keep in mind the benefits you receive from your partner and compare these benefits with the price you are paying for them.

Romantic Attraction as Motivation

When you are highly attracted to someone, the urge to please that person can motivate you to change your behavior. You may quit smoking when you had never been able to quit before, because your partner has asked you to stop. You may begin to like football, or may even become motivated to work on maturity problems that are standing in the way of having a more fulfilling relationship.

Sometimes the motivation goes into overdrive. *You* are so much in love with your partner that you don't read the red lights; you push yourself to see past the truth. Wistfully you think things will get better. Or you tell yourself, "We're so in love I can *change* those bad habits." Romantic attraction is a very strong force and it will often motivate a person to believe *anything* is possible.

But people rarely change on their own. Sometimes, if his or her love acts in therapeutic ways, the person will change; more often, the person will need a therapist in order to make a significant change. If the person who needs to change is as motivated to change as the person who desires the change, changes will be made. Mutual romantic attraction provides a strong incentive for an immature partner to grow up.

Using the Romantic Attraction Questionnaire

Most people have a good chance to have a happy and fulfilling lifetime love relationship.

The Love Test materials have been developed to help you accomplish this goal.

- Before you move in with your lover, you should consult The Love Test.
- Before you marry, you and your intended should use The Love Test materials.
- Before you divorce, you and your spouse should take these quizzes.
- Before you remarry, you and your intended should use these questionnaires.

In fact, you and your partner should test and then retest later. To make that easier for you, two complete sets of each quiz are included in this book. Because we recommend that you retest often, you can do so by using different-colored ink each time you take the tests.

The sixty statements in the Romantic Attraction Questionnaire are geared to measure the degree of excitement that characterizes an intimate relationship. When I say intimate, I don't mean sex alone; I mean total intimacy—good companionship in a relationship that will be the most important one in your life. The test statements, if rated honestly, will help you to determine your sense of excitement and desire for a permanent, close relationship with your partner. When you rate the statements as honestly as possible, you will be much more certain about how you feel.

In taking the test, rate how strongly you feel toward your partner/lover/spouse on each of the statements, awarding a 5 as the highest level of feeling and 1 as the lowest.

Scores can vary, so you should take the tests at least

twice—preferably three or more times. And save your first test scores so you can compare them to at least your second and third test scores. *Then,* if you find your test scores vary greatly from your own personal feelings, relax. You have probably not followed the directions properly.

Here's an example.

Gregg and Anita were about to marry. When they heard about The Love Test, they decided to confirm their feelings before the wedding. To their dismay, their Romantic Attraction Questionnaire scores were widely divergent and seemed to indicate they never should have connected.

When the three of us went through their answers, we found that Gregg never awarded a 5 to anyone, on anything. He was one of those people who had perfectionistic expectations and he thought a 3 was a respectable score. *Perfectionists* have difficulty making ratings because they tend to see 5 as perfect. In this book, 5 only means *very high*.

When they had a better understanding of the testing tools and retook the RAQ, Gregg and Anita learned that—as they had expected—their RAQ's were both high.

Semantic differences can also make for some distortion in rating a few of the items. Words and phrases may have slightly different meanings in different parts of the country.

Obviously, in order to score accurately, *you must understand the statement*. I have tried to make the statements as easy to understand as possible. But, invariably, students or patients tell me they don't understand a few of them.

If you come to a statement you don't understand, don't worry. Rate it a number 3. The rating scales have been developed so that a few middle scores of 3 will not affect your score in any significant way.

RAQ scores will usually vary little from rating to rating (provided you have not tested during an infatuation period), but mood may affect your test scores.

Avoid rating when you are in the dumps, mad at your lover, or feeling the pressures of the workaday world a bit too heavily. When you find your ratings have become consistent, you will know your scores are stable.

If you and your spouse are at war or have separated, rate your romantic attraction as you remember it during the good old days at the peak of your romance, after the infatuation period was past. If your partner is not available to score your emotional maturity, ask a friend or family member to rate you. Or you can rate yourself, if there is no one else who can.

The Love Test is not a test you pass or fail. There are no right or wrong answers. The questions are only a way of measuring feelings or behavior. As long as you rate these statements honestly, these materials can lead you to a better understanding of what is wrong and what you can do to improve your romantic involvement. The rest is up to you.

ROMANTIC ATTRACTION QUESTIONNAIRE

Instructions: Rate how strongly you feel toward your partner/lover/spouse on each of the following sixty statements. Circle one of the five numbers to the right of each statement, with 5 indicating the strongest feeling and 1 indicating the weakest. *Circle one number for each statement.* Each statement must be rated; if you are unsure of an answer or do not understand the statement, circle 3.

Each partner should fill out a Romantic Attraction Questionnaire.

Each partner can retest at a future date on the original questionnaire by using a different-colored ink.

Date_____ Rater_____

Total Score_____ Partner_____

	Low			High	
1. I feel very lucky to know this person.	1	2	3	4	5
2. I felt like there was something unusual and very special between us at our very first meeting.	1	2	3	4	5
3. We often have a very good time even when we are not doing anything special.	1	2	3	4	5
4. I miss this person a great deal when we are apart.	1	2	3	4	5
5. This person's approval is very important to me.	1	2	3	4	5
6. I get a thrill from just looking at this person.	1	2	3	4	5
7. I want this relationship to be permanent.	1	2	3	4	5
8. I am happiest when we are together.	1	2	3	4	5
9. Being with this person is far more important to me than where we are or what we are doing.	1	2	3	4	5
10. I enjoy this person in many ways other than just sharing affection.	1	2	3	4	5
11. I feel that we were meant for each other.	1	2	3	4	5
12. My friend is a beautiful person.	1	2	3	4	5
13. I enjoy planning things that we will be doing together.	1	2	3	4	5
14. I am curious about why and how much this person is interested in me.	1	2	3	4	5
15. I want our attraction to be mutual.	1	2	3	4	5
16. I am no longer looking for another romantic partner.	1	2	3	4	5
17. I get something very special from this person that I do not experience with anyone else.	1	2	3	4	5
18. I am willing to keep this relationship even if my friend makes no changes.	1	2	3	4	5
19. I love to surprise this person with a card or gift.	1	2	3	4	5

	Low			High	
20. I can forgive this person almost instantly.	1	2	3	4	5
21. I have a feeling of excitement when we are together.	1	2	3	4	5
22. I want to be very special in this person's life.	1	2	3	4	5
23. I would have to search for a long time to find someone I enjoy so much and so consistently.	1	2	3	4	5
24. Physical affection with this person is something very different and very special.	1	2	3	4	5
25. This person is a great companion.	1	2	3	4	5
26. My friend has an attractive personality.	1	2	3	4	5
27. I like doing things for this person.	1	2	3	4	5
28. Our relationship has something that is splendid and very hard to find.	1	2	3	4	5
29. This person is often on my mind.	1	2	3	4	5
30. There is something almost mystical in our eye-to-eye contact.	1	2	3	4	5
31. I experience unusual and pleasantly exciting feelings when I am with this person.	1	2	3	4	5
32. I am very willing to continue this relationship in spite of all the unpleasantness.	1	2	3	4	5
33. When there are tasks to be done, I prefer that we do them together.	1	2	3	4	5
34. I have made efforts to change in order to be more pleasing to my friend.	1	2	3	4	5
35. I enjoy discussing a wide variety of subjects with this person.	1	2	3	4	5
36. This is my most favorite person to be with.	1	2	3	4	5
37. We have something that could be described as spiritual intimacy.	1	2	3	4	5
38. I get a very pleasant sensation when I meet this person unexpectedly.	1	2	3	4	5

		Low			*High*	
39.	I would feel jealous if my friend became strongly interested in another person.	1	2	3	4	5
40.	I am, or could easily become, totally committed to this relationship.	1	2	3	4	5
41.	I enjoy being with this person even when we are silent.	1	2	3	4	5
42.	I want this person to respect me for my abilities.	1	2	3	4	5
43.	When things are going well between us I have a feeling of completeness and well-being.	1	2	3	4	5
44.	It means a lot to me when my friend does something special for me.	1	2	3	4	5
45.	At times I wish my friend would know me and accept me completely.	1	2	3	4	5
46.	I would like to know what my friend finds attractive about me.	1	2	3	4	5
47.	I like to touch and be touched by this person.	1	2	3	4	5
48.	I am attracted in a way that others do not understand.	1	2	3	4	5
49.	There are so many things I wish we could do together, if only there was enough time.	1	2	3	4	5
50.	If criticized by others, I would defend my friend.	1	2	3	4	5
51.	I am quite willing to do things for my friend without having to know the reason why.	1	2	3	4	5
52.	I have a protective interest about my friend's well-being.	1	2	3	4	5
53.	The pleasure I get from this relationship is well worth the price I pay.	1	2	3	4	5
54.	This person has a great deal of influence over me.	1	2	3	4	5
55.	I often wonder what my friend is thinking.	1	2	3	4	5

		Low			High	
56.	It's hard for me to say no to this person.	1	2	3	4	5
57.	I like to think up special surprises for my friend.	1	2	3	4	5
58.	I am happy when this person is pleased with me.	1	2	3	4	5
59.	This relationship is my strongest interest in life.	1	2	3	4	5
60.	This is the person with whom I would prefer to grow old.	1	2	3	4	5

To obtain the Total Score, add up all of the circled scores. Enter this score on the first page.

ROMANTIC ATTRACTION QUESTIONNAIRE

Instructions: Rate how strongly you feel toward your partner/lover/spouse on each of the following sixty statements. Circle one of the five numbers to the right of each statement, with 5 indicating the strongest feeling and 1 indicating the weakest. *Circle one number for each statement.* Each statement must be rated; if you are unsure of an answer or do not understand the statement, circle 3.

Each partner should fill out a Romantic Attraction Questionnaire.

Each partner can retest at a future date on the original questionnaire by using a different-colored ink.

Date_____ Rater_____

Total Score_____ Partner_____

	Low			High	
1. I feel very lucky to know this person.	1	2	3	4	5
2. I felt like there was something unusual and very special between us at our very first meeting.	1	2	3	4	5

		Low				High
3.	We often have a very good time even when we are not doing anything special.	1	2	3	4	5
4.	I miss this person a great deal when we are apart.	1	2	3	4	5
5.	This person's approval is very important to me.	1	2	3	4	5
6.	I get a thrill from just looking at this person.	1	2	3	4	5
7.	I want this relationship to be permanent.	1	2	3	4	5
8.	I am happiest when we are together.	1	2	3	4	5
9.	Being with this person is far more important to me than where we are or what we are doing.	1	2	3	4	5
10.	I enjoy this person in many ways other than just sharing affection.	1	2	3	4	5
11.	I feel that we were meant for each other.	1	2	3	4	5
12.	My friend is a beautiful person.	1	2	3	4	5
13.	I enjoy planning things that we will be doing together.	1	2	3	4	5
14.	I am curious about why and how much this person is interested in me.	1	2	3	4	5
15.	I want our attraction to be mutual.	1	2	3	4	5
16.	I am no longer looking for another romantic partner.	1	2	3	4	5
17.	I get something very special from this person that I do not experience with anyone else.	1	2	3	4	5
18.	I am willing to keep this relationship even if my friend makes no changes.	1	2	3	4	5
19.	I love to surprise this person with a card or gift.	1	2	3	4	5
20.	I can forgive this person almost instantly.	1	2	3	4	5
21.	I have a feeling of excitement when we are together.	1	2	3	4	5

	Low			High	

22. I want to be very special in this person's life.   1   2   3   4   5

23. I would have to search for a long time to find someone I enjoy so much and so consistently.   1   2   3   4   5

24. Physical affection with this person is something very different and very special.   1   2   3   4   5

25. This person is a great companion.   1   2   3   4   5

26. My friend has an attractive personality.   1   2   3   4   5

27. I like doing things for this person.   1   2   3   4   5

28. Our relationship has something that is splendid and very hard to find.   1   2   3   4   5

29. This person is often on my mind.   1   2   3   4   5

30. There is something almost mystical in our eye-to-eye contact.   1   2   3   4   5

31. I experience unusual and pleasantly exciting feelings when I am with this person.   1   2   3   4   5

32. I am very willing to continue this relationship in spite of all the unpleasantness.   1   2   3   4   5

33. When there are tasks to be done, I prefer that we do them together.   1   2   3   4   5

34. I have made efforts to change in order to be more pleasing to my friend.   1   2   3   4   5

35. I enjoy discussing a wide variety of subjects with this person.   1   2   3   4   5

36. This is my most favorite person to be with.   1   2   3   4   5

37. We have something that could be described as spiritual intimacy.   1   2   3   4   5

38. I get a very pleasant sensation when I meet this person unexpectedly.   1   2   3   4   5

39. I would feel jealous if my friend became strongly interested in another person.   1   2   3   4   5

	Low			High	

40. I am, or could easily become, totally committed to this relationship.   1 2 3 4 5

41. I enjoy being with this person even when we are silent.   1 2 3 4 5

42. I want this person to respect me for my abilities.   1 2 3 4 5

43. When things are going well between us I have a feeling of completeness and well-being.   1 2 3 4 5

44. It means a lot to me when my friend does something special for me.   1 2 3 4 5

45. At times I wish my friend would know me and accept me completely.   1 2 3 4 5

46. I would like to know what my friend finds attractive about me.   1 2 3 4 5

47. I like to touch and be touched by this person.   1 2 3 4 5

48. I am attracted in a way that others do not understand.   1 2 3 4 5

49. There are so many things I wish we could do together, if only there was enough time.   1 2 3 4 5

50. If criticized by others, I would defend my friend.   1 2 3 4 5

51. I am quite willing to do things for my friend without having to know the reason why.   1 2 3 4 5

52. I have a protective interest about my friend's well-being.   1 2 3 4 5

53. The pleasure I get from this relationship is well worth the price I pay.   1 2 3 4 5

54. This person has a great deal of influence over me.   1 2 3 4 5

55. I often wonder what my friend is thinking.   1 2 3 4 5

56. It's hard for me to say no to this person.   1 2 3 4 5

	Low			*High*	
57. I like to think up special surprises for my friend.	1	2	3	4	5
58. I am happy when this person is pleased with me.	1	2	3	4	5
59. This relationship is my strongest interest in life.	1	2	3	4	5
60. This is the person with whom I would prefer to grow old.	1	2	3	4	5

To obtain the Total Score, add up all of the circled scores. Enter this score on the first page.

How to Interpret Your RAQ Scores

The Romantic Attraction Questionnaire measures the degree of interest, excitement, or desire that one person feels toward another. Its focus is on the person-to-person factor and doesn't attempt to measure sexual interest. Often sexual interest exists without a genuine sense of excitement toward that person as a longtime companion. Almost invariably, when there is a strong romantic attraction, there is also a strong interest in sharing affection and sex.

The Romantic Attraction Questionnaire doesn't differentiate between genuine, long-lasting romantic interest and infatuation. Research strongly suggests that as many as six out of seven times a strong romantic interest can evaporate or be turned off permanently within three to four months. However, when the romantic interest remains strong longer than a period of four months, it almost invariably persists for a great many years. (There can be exceptions to this general rule. Often, after a commitment of marriage or its equivalent is made and the "honeymoon is over," a fear of closeness can disrupt or weaken a relationship. Love can "disappear," loss of sexual interest and/or extramarital affairs can all be *symptoms of someone being afraid to be close*.)

This four-month period can serve to test between

mere infatuation and genuine romantic interest only if there is frequent contact. The mere passage of time or minimal involvement, such as through correspondence, are not valid measures. Fantasy romances carried on by mail can last for years only to end in a few days when there is real, flesh-and-blood, personal contact. So, only time, and not the Romantic Attraction Questionnaire, will tell if the excitement will be lasting or not.

Another factor to be considered before trying to interpret RAQ scores is that the Romantic Attraction Questionnaire can be sensitive to our moods. For example, if we are angry, sad, or frightened, then our ratings could fluctuate as much as twenty or thirty points. Thus, we may register a relatively low score because of our present mood. The next day we could rate our sentiments much higher. Therefore, if your score doesn't seem to agree with your longer term evaluation of your degree of interest, you should rerate.

If you feel a strong emotion has colored your choices and your score is borderline, you will want to rerate your Romantic Attraction Questionnaire. When reratings are made, they should be done with different-colored pens and the mood and date noted.

With these conditional factors in mind, you are now ready to interpret your score.

Score Ranges

260–300	Romantic attraction is very strong
220–260	Romantic attraction is strong
200–220	Romantic attraction is borderline
180–200	Romantic attraction is weak
Below 180	Little, if any, romantic interest

Since 60 is the lowest possible score and 300 is the highest, extreme scores are relatively simple to interpret. Scores below 180 mean there is little, if any, romantic interest, as is found in one or both partners in the middle and bottom rows of the Love Relationships

Chart (see p. 3). These types of relationships are not likely to work out. There must be a relatively strong mutual romantic interest (and reasonably high emotional maturity) for things to work out well for the couple, no matter how hard they may try.

Scores below 200 are weak, and scores between 200 and 220 indicate borderline interest.

Scores of 220 and above are almost always ˙ high enough for the relationship to be very satisfying.

If both you and your partner have scores of 220 or above, then your relationship will be found in the top row of the Love Relationships chart, because you have strong mutual attraction.

If one of your scores is over 220 and the other is below 200, then your relationship will be one of the three in the second row of the Love Relationships chart. Relationships in this middle row reflect a one-way attraction. There is little chance of things working out happily unless the low scorer is not very far below 200. Obviously, the greater the difference between your scores, the less chance there is for a very satisfying relationship. Unfortunately, while we know how to improve emotional maturity, no one knows how to create romantic excitement that does not already exist or how to erase those feelings when they do exist.

If you both score below 200 consistently, then you should be looking for other partners. However, that doesn't mean you cannot remain friends. In fact, when there is mutually low romantic interest, it is much easier to have a satisfying and long-lasting friendship.

Should both my partner and I use the RAQ? Should we make repeated ratings?

Occasionally I have students who never take these materials to their partners. Instead, they rate their own feelings in the RAQ and realize that such feelings are not high enough to sustain a relationship with their current lover. They break up and move on to other relationships.

While this can and does work well for some people,

each person will benefit more from The Love Test if *each partner* rates both aspects of love: romantic attraction and emotional maturity. One person can rate his or her feelings for the other, but the problems and solutions pertinent to a relationship can only become more clear when both partners make both ratings. This way, you make sure that some deficiency will not go unrecognized or interfere in your next relationship.

It is important to make repeated ratings on the RAQ. Assuming that a first rating gives an accurate picture can be dangerous. Sometimes the first rating is the highest or lowest of a group of ratings made over several weeks' time. The range between the average and the highest of the repeated ratings is most likely to be the truest measure of romantic interest.

Can your romantic attraction for someone change over the years? Will your RAQ scores change for the better over time?

No. Once you're talking about true romantic attraction and not infatuation, the RAQ usually remains quite consistent over the years. The passionate interest this test measures changes very little and doesn't seem to be gained or lost. There will be temporary fluctuations due to mood and good or bad treatment, but, over time, romantic attraction scores on the RAQ will typically vary less than ten points in one direction or the other, after a stable base-line score has been determined.

RAQ is like an IQ (Intelligence Quotient). The IQ is basically determined by your inborn genetic endowment. It's like height; some people are born with the potential to be five feet six inches. IQ measures our capacity to solve new and complex problems rapidly and accurately. Romantic attraction measures our capacity to respond more to Jane than to Mary, or more to Joe than to Pete. It's a biopsychological energy that's inborn—a response potential.

Through the years Freud and others have thought that romantic attraction was a culturally determined matter. I don't agree. It has been thought that romantic love is the quest for the complete love with mother, for the relationship we never had with her. T that its basic nature is neurosis. I don't believe attraction is a neurotic response.

A difference between romantic excitement and the RAQ score can occur. Sometimes a low score is not a true reflection of the romantic attraction you feel for another person because your true feelings are masked by mood or negative experiences. Excitement can be lessened by disappointment, fear, anger, or other unpleasant kinds of experience. Actually, the romantic chemistry is still there, but it's getting more and more buried under a blanket of negative emotions. Sometimes partners will make a mistake and divorce each other for the wrong reason at this point in the relationship. However, if there is the necessary insight and commitment to change, backed up by real change, then the romantic excitement can resurface and the partners will fall in love all over again—and the RAQ scores will again be high.

Sometimes wide swings in RAQ scores simply reflect the immaturity of the rater. Emotionally immature people are more prone to react in extreme ways to life's experiences. In such cases, repeated ratings will provide a more accurate average RAQ score.

If you had true love but you sort of lost it, can it come back?

Yes, definitely—if you've had true romantic excitement and not infatuation. When it is a case of infatuation, typically the initial high RAQ scores will drop sharply within the first three to four months. Occasionally, the RAQ scores will drop less sharply, but the RAQ scores will never return to their former high levels.

The degree of emotional maturity of the rater can introduce RAQ score fluctuations; a mature rater has less variation among repeated scores than does an immature rater.

You never "lose" true romantic attraction; it just becomes buried when your partner mistreats or neglects ɔu. You may believe that you have "fallen out of love." Often this is wrong. One way to check and to be more sure that you have a clear understanding of your degree of romantic interest in your partner is to think back to a time, after the infatuation time period has definitely passed, when your romantic interest was at its peak. This will show you, by rating how you felt then, what is possible in the future if you and your partner work at improving your relationship.

If RAQ scores were once higher, the couple can work to improve their relationship and "rediscover" their romantic attraction for each other.

One of the items on the Romantic Attraction Questionnaire asks if you can easily forgive this person. If you can, that's a strong indicator that there's a lot of romantic excitement going on deep inside of you. If you see hope, you forgive this person and hope that your lover is genuine and sincere, that he or she really is changing, and that things will get better. As things improve, your original romantic attraction will resurface.

Chapter Three

♡　♡　♡

Emotional Maturity: What It Is and How to Measure it

Emotional maturity is the second key—and even slightly more important than romantic attraction—to the happiness of your love relationship.

Divorce statistics and the numbers of people going for counseling indicate that an estimated thirty to fifty million people in this country alone suffer in their love relationships. That's about twenty percent of the total United States population. Some of these people have problems because they are involved with someone who doesn't share their high degree of romantic attraction. Many of these people have problems because they don't have a high enough maturity level to deal with the responsibilities of a successful relationship.

A good number of these individuals suffer from problems in both areas. To have the kind of lasting love we're talking about in an idealized fashion, you need to have a sufficient amount of both maturity and romantic attraction. If the romantic attraction is not there, nothing can be done to create it; we know that. But if emotional maturity is missing, the relationship need not be abandoned. Romantic attraction *cannot* be acquired; emotional maturity *can* be acquired. Maturity comprises *learned* skills.

There are, unfortunately, some people who are so immature they think they're mature. These people seldom mature emotionally because they seldom seek help. They are quick to blame others for their problems and they cannot see deeply enough into themselves to recognize a need for change. Occasionally, they may fall so in love with someone that they will be made to realize they'll have to shape up in order to keep the relationship.

The Mature Person

Emotional maturity refers to the areas and degrees to which a person is making a successful adjustment to life. The emotionally mature person has good mental health. All this person needs for a good relationship is another person with a reasonably high RAQ score and enough emotional maturity.

Emotionally mature people are able to cope with life's problems and challenges. They are readily in touch with their own feelings and those of other people. They cope well in a wide variety of emotionally charged situations even when fearful, angry, frustrated, or disappointed. They can ask for a raise or accept being laid off without weeks of worry or recrimination. Emotionally mature people are in touch with reality; they may have fantasies, but they are not walking around in a dream world.

They have good insight into their own motivations. In relating to others, mature people behave in positive and constructive ways. They care about the well-being of others, recognize other people's worth, and treat others with consideration, inclusion, and respect. They call their mothers on Mother's Day. They readily make and keep friends. They share in decision making and resolve conflicts constructively.

They take initiative and responsibility when appropriate; they plan for the future, are organized, self-reliant, and are good at problem solving. They have good self-control, are patient, reasonably neat, persevering, and willing to do their share of the work. If the dishwasher is broken, they will know where to find the warranty and will make the effort to call the dealer and to be home when the repairperson arrives. They are honest, sincere, fair, and can accept blame when at fault.

If your relationship is not working because of one or more immaturity problems, The Love Test will offer guidance on methods that are helping other people improve their relationships. In most cases of maturity problems, at least some professional guidance is needed. Look carefully at all four of the different areas of emotional growth that comprise maturity—awareness, relating, competence, and integrity—and consider whether low maturity in certain traits might be hurting your relationship.

When we are **aware,** we know what we are feeling, thinking, and doing. As little children, we are aware, knowing the pleasures of holding and playing with a spoon, or watching mother doing all those fascinating things, moving from one place to another. We also knew the unpleasant feelings of being cold or wet, hungry or neglected. As we grew older, a great deal of attention was paid to our behavior.

Our entire culture is focused on behavior: what we can or cannot do at home, what we must or must not do at school, where and when we can or cannot do things in the neighborhood, what we must do to get a job and not do to keep it. It's always been behavior. We are a nation of movers and doers. We are action oriented.

But we are basically feeling creatures, at all times inclined toward gaining pleasure or avoiding pain or discomfort, although these feelings are much less discussed than is behavior. So, in time, as part of our cultural indoctrination, we suppress our feelings more and more. When we are asked, "How are you feeling?" we've learned that really means "Hello." The other person doesn't mean that he or she is ready to sit down and listen to a fifteen-minute description of our good and bad feelings. But when we are asked, "What did you do?" then we know an answer is expected.

So we think about our actions, not about our feelings. Besides, feelings tend to be "vague, fuzzy things," often very difficult to describe. We may just shrug or grimace, and it all ends there. We don't learn how to study, understand, and give an articulate description of our feelings. To a great extent we grow up as emotional illiterates.

Feelings are at the core of our existence, our experience. We have good thoughts that arise from pleasant feelings and these thoughts can lead to some positive action. We have dark thoughts that arise from unpleasant feelings and we may take some negative action, break something that isn't working right, or we could take positive action and fix it so it works. If there were no feelings, there would probably not be much thought and very little behavior. The word *emotion* literally means to make move. We move because we feel, and just because we have lost touch with our feelings doesn't change the fact that feelings are the basic cause of all action.

The challenge of awareness means that we must make deliberate efforts to counter our cultural indoctrination. We must stop, listen, and *feel!*

John Donne observed that "No man is an *Island,* entire of it self"; we are all social beings. We need contact, association, and involvement with other people— what we call **relating;** the more meaningful and intimate, the more fulfilling. The relationship that usually provides the most avenues of meaning and fulfillment is that of the well-matched, mature lovers. This doesn't mean that our parents and children, friends and other associates don't provide us with important relationships. With the exception of people who are mutually involved in some exciting business, scientific research,

politics, or creative activity, the most important, i
and most broadly based relationship is the one
lover.

With a lover there is the opportunity to make a deep
emotional investment—to combine abilities, resources—
to form a strong partnership in which the whole is more
than the sum of its parts. Many believe that to form
such a union is to establish an unhealthy and morbid
dependency, to give up or surrender our individuality,
to lose our respective identities. But this is simply not
so. There is no reason why a person cannot be a deeply
committed team player and still remain very much his
or her own person apart from team functioning.

When you make a deep emotional investment and
commitment to your lover, you do give up a certain
degree of freedom of movement; we haven't yet learned
how to be in two places at once. This can and does
cause conflict, but not so much conflict that two mature
people cannot find a reasonable set of compromises.
Any couple can find a reasonable balance between time
together and time apart.

Another inescapable area of conflict is that of vulnerability. When we seek the romantic and caring interest
of another person, we want a lot from him or her, yet
each of our expectations makes us vulnerable to
disappointment. We want our lover to live, but death
can happen; we want our lover to be healthy, but illness
comes; we want our lover's attention, but there will
always be some neglect; we want approval, but can get
disapproval; we want meshing of moods and tastes, but
we can be out of sync. The needs and expectations form
a very strong list of possible rewards and possible
disappointments or frustrations.

Being vulnerable, it is only natural that we should
hedge our investment, develop a form of emotional
insurance so that when things do go wrong, as we know
they will, then all will not be lost. But as we hedge, we
distance our lovers; we reduce consciously or unconsciously the degree of our emotional investment. We
withdraw. And too often this withdrawal to a more

comfortable degree of investment is misunderstood, misinterpreted as rejection. The mature couple will discuss this mutual issue and reduce unnecessary hurt feelings. Understanding will replace false assumptions.

As a therapist, I have often been asked what closeness is. A definition that seems to have almost universal meaning has several basic aspects: (1) sharing intimate thoughts; (2) sharing intimate feelings; (3) discussing the daily issues of living; (4) discussing and solving problems together; (5) making decisions together; and (6) doing things together. As you relate to your partner in these ways, then closeness becomes only a matter of degree; the more you share in these aspects of life, the closer will be your relationship.

If you are both romantically interested and reasonably mature, then this kind of a close relationship will almost certainly turn out to be the most satisfying and fulfilling relationship of your life. The more you put into this relationship, if both of you are serious investors, then the more benefits will accrue.

Making a successful adjustment in life requires not only being aware and relating well to other people, but also being effective in dealing with the continuous stream of problems that challenge us in our everyday lives. **Competence,** or effectiveness, is literally our key to survival. Along with emotional blindness, emotional illiteracy, and loneliness, helplessness is another serious obstacle along our path to a fulfilling life.

The antidote for helplessness is competence. The challenge to become a competent person goes on throughout our lives; it doesn't end the day we leave school with a diploma in our hands. Competence requires hard work, plenty of practice, and the willingness to take on new challenges under ever-changing circumstances.

Integrity literally means being together, within ourselves. It means that our functioning fits very closely our ideal image of ourselves. It means that we live in a self-respecting manner, in ways that earn the respect of other people. Its two main determiners are self-discipline and ethical behavior. Karen Horney, one of the greatest contributors to understanding the inner workings of our minds, summed it all up when she said that we cannot like or respect ourselves when we do not behave in self-respecting ways. Her point is that though we may kid ourselves along at the conscious level, deep inside we know the truth. We don't really like ourselves or respect ourselves when we are not behaving as decent, moral people.

Self-discipline is gained only through taking on unpleasantness, challenge, and adversity. Yet our push-putton society has tended toward making many things too easy for us. Open the refrigerator door and there's the food; press the button on the TV or radio and out pops entertainment. Flip a switch and there is light. None of these life-made-easy comforts build the inner strengths of being willing and able to work hard, to endure unpleasantness, to be persevering, to exercise self-control, or to wait willingly for good things to happen.

Our culture's abuse of public relations, with all its pretentious image-making, has not been conducive to honesty, genuineness, or fairness. If we don't feel guilty when we belie the reality of another person, or take advantage of another, then we are undermining our society and our own consciences, our senses of moral decency. If we don't treat other people as we want them to treat us, then we can never have any genuine self-respect.

You Can't Tell Maturity by Age

There are among us the less adequate men and women of the world, who have grown up biologically but remain children in the emotional maturity department. Some people have been limited or crippled in child-hood by lack of attention or by parenting that was

critical, demanding, or punitive; or by a combina-
f neglect and oppression. They have entered the
n-up world as pseudoadults; in reality they are still
children who have only grown larger and have become
sexually developed. They appear to be grown-up, and
have been around long enough to give the appearance
of and at times behave as grown-ups.

However, the truth is that they are as children, their
childhood unfinished, unfulfilled, and their business in
life is chiefly to fulfill the deprivations of their child-
hoods. And sometimes, on top of that, to rectify the
injustices, to refight the lost battles of childhood, but
this time, if at all possible, to win.

In varying degrees, their deepest wish is to be taken
care of. Filled with self-doubt, they believe they cannot
cope with the uncertainties and demands of life. The
solution they seek is to find someone who either looks
strong or is believed to be strong by others.

Their self-esteem is low, sometimes very low. Genuine self-esteem is the product of building strong friend-
ships and leading a productive life. Only love and work
can build self-esteem. Love and productivity give us
value. If our parents give us enough loving, then we
will feel lovable. If they encourage us to develop our
abilities so that we can contribute to society, then we
will know that we are valuable. We will then have good
self-esteem.

Many of us, however, have had too little convincing
that we are lovable and capable and productive.
Hungering for those reassuring messages that have not
come, some of us have developed an opposite image of
ourselves. We feel somewhat deficient and unworthy.
We may be willing to enter into a state of emotional
dependency upon another person, and on that person's
terms.

However, as with everything else in life, being taken
care of has its price. For such a hoped-for guarantee may
mean accommodating to the partner's neglect or oppres-
sive demands. This may mean that the wife spends the

money any way she wishes to or that if the husban[d]
a mistress, well then those are the terms of the deal.

The female version of this child-appearing-as-adult
pattern has been called by Colette Dowling the Cinderella
complex. Here the woman foregoes the benefits and
responsibilities of being an emotionally mature person
for the compromise of being taken care of, especially
financially, but also being willing to be dominated
psychologically by her husband. She molds herself to
his desires, his interests, his vocational pursuits, his
choice of people with whom to associate and to entertain.

The male version of this child-appearing-as-adult syndrome might be called the Little Prince complex. Here,
usually the man is willing to work, but at that point in
responsibility he turns everything of consequence over
to his wife to decide, to be responsible for. In many
cases he just turns over his paycheck and thinks and
worries no more about how the relationship or its affairs
are handled. His attitude is, "I put the bread on the
table, now you take care of everything else." What this
really means is that he is willing to grow up to a large
extent in the competence department, but draws the
line there and will not take seriously the challenges of
growing up in awareness, relating, or integrity. In effect,
he becomes the little boy of his wife, neatly (he believes)
disguised as the big male provider for the family, dele-
gating all the "secondary" matters to his wife. He wants
her to take care of him emotionally, and often she does.
She makes the big decisions about where they live, how
the children are disciplined, how the money is spent,
and then "reports" (often resentfully) to her "man." He
is thus informed, and rubber stamps everything. Many
women rebel and say, "I'm not your mother."

It is important to keep in mind that there are two
kinds of relationships. In the healthy relationship there
is mutual liking, respect, and trust. In the unhealthy
relationship the closeness is in reality some kind of a
neurotic bargain, characterized by feelings of futility
and safety mechanisms. Only the mature relationship

will yield the rewards of true intimacy, of mutual affection, respect, and trust, culminating in many years of enriching companionship.

Some Common Patterns of Immaturity

Karen Horney, in her classic book *Neurosis and Human Growth*, carefully describes the three most typical patterns of immaturity seen in our culture. She describes them as the domineering type, the self-effacing type, and the avoiders.

The Domineering Type

The domineering type is the ego-tripper, the person so insecure that he or she must control every relationship, or he or she won't become involved at all. Such persons seek power either through rank, money, or both. Their basic outlook is that people will take advantage of you any time you allow them the chance. They cannot trust, and they are determined always to beat the other fellow to the draw. They see every relationship as a contest, a battleground, a chess game. In this person's world, there are no people other than winners or losers.

The Self-effacing Type

The self-effacing person is the one who is always apologizing. As he or she sees it, nothing is ever done well enough. Such people feel weak, inadequate, and very unsure of themselves. They operate under the assumption that any other person's opinion is probably superior. They seek affiliation, but are always willing to have companionship on the other person's terms. Often they will mesh with the domineering type because of the mutual meeting of needs. This couple has what is sometimes called the master-slave relationship.

The Avoiders

The avoidistic type of person has never had a close relationship, or if as a child he or she was close to someone, it was devoid of attention, filled with criticism and punishment. Their guiding philosophy is that if they don't get close, their expectations of attention won't be disappointed and they certainly won't hurt as much if they are criticized or punished. So they keep their distance. Yet they are often found at the periphery of emotional involvement, wistfully hoping that some person will approach them, take the first risks of intimacy, give abundant reassurance, make them feel safe enough to begin to relate. I once had a very dramatic experience in leading a group discussion of seventy-five people who had met once a week, year in and year out. Most of them had been members for five years or more. I was amazed to find out that their common, universal complaint was that no one ever approached them and told them who they were and how they really felt about things. After a short period, to a person they realized that they were all waiting for the other person to approach them first. Of course, nothing happened. No relationships were formed, and they all still had their "safe distance," and no relationships.

Should you wait for your own maturity to develop before you begin to look for a serious love partner?

Both can and should be done together. Maturation goes best when you are involved with a caring person with whom there is reasonably strong mutual romantic attraction.

One way to get a more objective evaluation of your emotional maturity is to have at least three other people who know you very well rate you independently on the Emotional Maturity Rating Form. You can also rate yourself. When you look at the scores, you will know a great deal more about your emotional maturity and what areas need further efforts and improvement.

If more than one-third of the scores in any one area are very low, then you are not very mature in that area.

The most mature people have the most successful lives and the most successful marriages (although luck and health also figure in!), so it behooves you to gain as much emotional maturity as possible.

Can you spot a loser before getting involved?

Unless you have observed a person closely in another relationship, you can't spot a loser *before* you get involved. You have to have had at least a minimal association with the person first. It can often take a long time to get to know many important things about another person. All you can tell for sure in the beginning is your degree of excitement about this person. It doesn't take long to figure out whether you are excited about a person or not. While it might be infatuation rather than true romantic excitement, after several months you will know if it's the real thing. Repeated ratings on the RAQ will help you spot an infatuation. However, you have to know a person reasonably well before you can make positive or negative decisions about that person's personality and character.

When should you move in with someone?

Not before 90 to 120 days of really getting to know one another. In fact, I recommend you don't even try to rate the person on the Emotional Maturity Rating Form until after you've known your partner for several months. You've got to know that person well enough to be able to answer the questions accurately. And never move in together without first using The Love Test materials.

Moving in together is not a lot different from being married. If you live together and find that you are suffering from infatuation, you're going to be moving out. That can be a big problem. Remember, it's much easier to get involved than it is to get uninvolved. If you don't know the person well enough to make the ratings, you don't know him or her well enough to become seriously involved.

You don't have to live together to use The Love Test. You should spend a lot of time together so you can tell the difference between infatuation and real chemistry. If a person's behavior is turning you off rapidly, then it's probably not romantic chemistry. You can spend time together two, three, or four times a week without living together and, in this way, get to know each other.

If someone is acting, that act can't go on indefinitely. Occasionally, you may meet someone with a Jekyll and Hyde personality and the flip side may not show up for years. That is just one of the risks.

And people who are close to one another still perceive things differently. When three adolescent children each independently rated the emotional maturity of their father, there was a fair amount of agreement about the strong and weak points of his maturity. Yet there were some notable differences. The differences were not due to distortion but rather to the differing relationships the children had with their father. One was the favored child and spent the most time with his father. The second child shared an intellectual relationship that centered around problem-solving activities and achievement. The third child was messy, so he saw his father as a strict disciplinarian and a much more self-disciplined man than the other children believed him to be. Actually, the father *was* a slightly different person with each child. So differences in scores can reflect differences in relationships. You can and should rate a person only as *you* perceive him or her. How he or she behaves in other situations with other people is not now of primary concern; however, it is another dimension of personality that could sooner or later affect your relationship.

Factors That Influence Your Ratings

There are several factors that could influence your rating of another person's emotional maturity, so keep them in mind before you begin to rate.

Your own emotional maturity. Emotionally mature people make more objective ratings than immature people. They tend to have fewer distortions, and several ratings over a period of time will cluster together closely. If you believe your partner's ratings of you are distorted (this usually means downgraded), have three other people rate you independently of each other. If your partner rates you low in traits that others who know you well all agree should be much higher, you can put greater belief in the scores of that group of people who agrees. Discuss these comparisons with your partner. Try to resolve discrepancies, then ask your partner to rerate you. If you still can't resolve the discrepancy, a few sessions together with a counselor should clarify the ratings' differences.

Mood. Everyone is likely to be more generous in rating when enjoying a good mood. This is easily corrected by making repeated ratings and looking for the pattern or average.

Misunderstanding the directions. Misunderstanding the directions is the most common reason for "wrong" scores. If you see that your ratings of your partner don't tally at all with your perception of him or her, go back through the instructions and rerate.

The rater is a perfectionist. On rare occasions, the person making the rating will be a severe perfectionist and will not give a "very often" to anyone. To the extreme perfectionist, only God gets a "very often." Perfectionists should be encouraged to loosen up and relax before rerating and they will usually give more reasonable scores.

The lovers have been at war. If one or both partners

are angry at each other, there will be a tendency to downgrade one another. The more immature the partner, the more downgrading. This is best corrected by having the angry person rerate the partner's behavior in terms of a time when the relationship was going well.

Stress. Stress, illness, being overtired or overworked can influence your ratings.

Falsification

In my practice, I have found it uncommon for people to cheat on either part of The Love Test. However, since it is possible to falsify your ratings, let's discuss the two types of falsification.

Deliberate falsification is rare and I'm not sure of the reason why. I think it is because people realize that if they falsify their ratings, they will not find out what's really going on in their relationship. On the very infrequent occasions when I have seen emotional maturity ratings falsified, they have always been done by someone who has a very controlling and manipulative personality, the type of person who is a supreme game player who must control every situation because he or she trusts no one.

Subconscious falsification is more common because the person making the mistaken rating really believes that he is seeing and rating the truth. One man who was extremely frightened of a close relationship and who could only feel safe when he was agreed with, rated his patner (which whom he had a very high RAQ) as being immature in terms of her insight and relating ability. This is a classic case of projection. The rater himself has problems in relating but cannot admit to them, so he projects them onto someone else close to him. When his partner had three of her close friends rate her, they were all in agreement that she had considerable insight into her own motivation and that she related quite well.

Using the Emotional Maturity Rating Form

There are two copies of the EMRF so that you and your partner may both rate each other on the sixty-three behavioral traits of emotional maturity. Place both scores on the first page of your EMRF and then fill in your Personal Love Profile (p. 102). Then take a look at the Love Relationships Chart (p. 3). Remember that maturity can and will grow if the necessary efforts are made. Rerate frequently. It's just possible you can have the relationship you dream of!

EMOTIONAL MATURITY RATING FORM

Instructions: Rate your partner/lover/spouse on each of these sixty-three behavioral traits in terms of how often his behavior is observed by you, almost never (*an*); sometimes (*s*); moderately often (*mo*); often (*o*); very often (*vo*). When possible, rate this person's behavior when with you or relating to you. Every item must be rated. Circle the letter code which most accurately describes your partner's behavior. If you do not understand the statement, circle *mo*. Add up the number of ratings that you circled on the left-hand side of the stripe. These low scores should be totaled in each of the four major areas of maturity. Enter these scores on the lines below. Each of these low ratings show a probable area of immaturity.

Date_____ Rater_____
Maturity Scores_____ Partner_____
Number of Low Awareness Scores _____
Number of Low Relating Scores _____
Number of Low Competence Scores _____
Number of Low Integrity Scores _____

	almost never	sometimes	moderately often	often	very often

Awareness

1. *Knowing your own feelings*
   My friend is aware of and able to report his or her own feelings with accuracy.

	an	s	mo	o	vo

2. *Knowing the feelings of others*
   My friend is sensitive to and can accurately describe the feelings other people have.

	an	s	mo	o	vo

3. *Being spontaneously expressive*
   My friend is emotionally expressive in a natural and immediate way.

	an	s	mo	o	vo

4. *Ability to discuss personal feelings*
   My friend is able to discuss personal feelings with accuracy and is willing to do so.

	an	s	mo	o	vo

5. *Coping with mixed feelings*
   My friend accepts the inevitability of having mixed feelings and copes effectively with them.

	an	s	mo	o	vo

6. *Curiosity*
   My friend's behavior is inquisitive and investigative.

	an	s	mo	o	vo

	almost never	sometimes	moderately often	often	very often

Awareness (cont.)

7. *Getting desires met constructively*
   My friend's personal desires and needs are met in constructive ways.

	an	s	mo	o	vo

8. *Coping with fear*
   My friend is aware of his or her fearful feelings, but copes with the situation in effective ways.

	an	s	mo	o	vo

9. *Coping with anger*
   My friend is aware of his or her feelings of anger, but copes with the situation in effective ways.

	an	s	mo	o	vo

10. *Accepting responsibility for failure*
    My friend undefensively recognizes and accepts his or her own limitations when they are the cause of failure.

	an	s	mo	o	vo

11. *Coping with frustration and discouragement*
    My friend is positive, persistent, and effective in resolving feelings of frustration and discouragement.

	an	s	mo	o	vo

	almost never	sometimes	moderately often	often	very often

Awareness (cont.)

12. *Accepting and approving of self*
My friend freely acknowledges personal limitations and still feels acceptable and worthy

	an	s	mo	o	vo

13. *Coping with uncertainty*
My friend accepts some degree of uncertainty as inevitable and retains a positive and willing attitude about dealing with it.

	an	s	mo	o	vo

14. *Sorting out real and make-believe*
My friend readily distinguishes reality, knowing clearly the difference between the real and make-believe.

	an	s	mo	o	vo

15. *Using imagination constructively*
My friend displays a well-developed imagination and applies these ideas in constructive ways.

	an	s	mo	o	vo

Number of Low Awareness Scores _____

Relating

	almost never	sometimes	moderately often	often	very often
1. *Caring about others* My friend is sensitive and constructively responsive to the needs of others.	an	s	mo	o	vo
2. *Getting attention constructively* My friend gets his or her needs for attention met in constructive ways.	an	s	mo	o	vo
3. *Earning acceptance* My friend wins acceptance and inclusion by respecting the values of others.	an	s	mo	o	vo
4. *Earning approval from others* My friend earns recognition and praise from others.	an	s	mo	o	vo
5. *Giving affectionate regard* My friend demonstrates warm personal interest in other people.	an	s	mo	o	vo
6. *Being socially responsible* My friend understands his or her ability to affect people for better or for worse and uses this power responsibly.	an	s	mo	o	vo

Relating (cont.)	almost never	sometimes	moderately often	often	very often
7. *Being considerate* My friend is aware of other people's feelings and deals with them in considerate ways.	an	s	mo	o	vo
8. *Making friends* My friend makes friends easily and keeps them.	an	s	mo	o	vo
9. *Coping with peer pressure* My friend is able to resist negative peer pressure.	an	s	mo	o	vo
10. *Expressing dissatisfaction constructively* My friend is able to express complaints or criticism in ways that are supportive of the other person.	an	s	mo	o	vo
11. *Reciprocating good treatment* My friend recognizes, appreciates, and voluntarily reciprocates good treatment.	an	s	mo	o	vo
12. *Sharing in decision making* My friend lives by the value of obtaining and giving others an equal voice in the decision-making process.	an	s	mo	o	vo

Relating (cont.)

	almost never	sometimes	moderately often	often	very often
13. **Keeping promises** My friend keeps his or her promises.	an	s	mo	o	vo
14. **Resolving conflicts constructively** My friend, without sacrificing his or her own rights, uses peaceful and constructive means for resolving conflicts.	an	s	mo	o	vo
15. **Willingness to share** My friend willingly shares recognition and possessions.	an	s	mo	o	vo
16. **Becoming more likable** My friend appreciates and constructively uses criticism in order to become a more likable person.	an	s	mo	o	vo
17. **Coping with mixed feelings toward people** My friend recognizes, accepts, and deals constructively in disappointments and disagreements with other people.	an	s	mo	o	vo
18. **Responding well to opposite sex** My friend is equally courteous to members of both sexes.	an	s	mo	o	vo

Number of Low Relating Scores _____

Competence	almost never	sometimes	moderately often	often	very often
1. *Applying energy and effort* My friend is willing to apply energy and effort.	an	s	mo	o	vo
2. *Using knowledge and skills* My friend demonstrates that he or she has acquired knowledge and skills.	an	s	mo	o	vo
3. *Being planful* My friend behaves in planful and organized ways	an	s	mo	o	vo
4. *Showing initiative* My friend initiates and implements ideas and projects.	an	s	mo	o	vo
5. *Showing creativity* My friend demonstrates original and inventive ways of doing things.	an	s	mo	o	vo
6. *Behaving with realistic expectations* My friend's expectations and goals are realistic.	an	s	mo	o	vo
7. *Showing self-reliance* My friend relies upon his or her own resources to meet objectives.	an	s	mo	o	vo

Competence (cont.)	almost never	sometimes	moderately often	often	very often
8. *Willingly takes on challenge* My friend is willing and eager to try his or her abilities with new tasks.	an	s	mo	o	vo
9. *Showing appropriate caution* My friend anticipates and avoids serious dangers.	an	s	mo	o	vo
10. *Showing self-confidence* My friend shows an attitude of assurance when coping with new situations.	an	s	mo	o	vo
11. *Being responsible* My friend, without being reminded, fulfills obligations.	an	s	mo	o	vo
12. *Being motivated to succeed* My friend shows interest in and motivation for success.	an	s	mo	o	vo
13. *Being goal-directed* My friend has highly defined goals that are pursued constructively.	an	s	mo	o	vo
14. *Showing high standards* My friend values and pursues high levels of accuracy and skill in his or her work.	an	s	mo	o	vo

	almost never	sometimes	moderately often	often	very often

Competence (cont.)

15. *Being cooperative*
My friend combines his
or her talents well with
those of others to achieve
a common benefit.

	an	s	mo	o	vo

16. *Showing flexibility*
My friend is willing to
consider new informa-
tion and try new ways
under changing circum-
stances in order to
pursue the same original
goal.

	an	s	mo	o	vo

17. *Developing personal
interests*
My friend has strong
personal interests and
pursues them.

	an	s	mo	o	vo

18. *Solving problems
effectively*
My friend is organized
and effective in his or
her problem-solving
methods.

	an	s	mo	o	vo

Number of Low Competence Scores ____

Integrity

1. *Showing self-control*
My friend's controls pre-
vail over impulse.

	an	s	mo	o	vo

Integrity (cont.)

	almost never	sometimes	moderately often	often	very often
2. Waiting willingly My friend waits with a realistic and calm attitude.	an	s	mo	o	vo
3. Being truthful in statements My friend is natural, spontaneous, and sincere when describing events.	an	s	mo	o	vo
4. Coping with unpleasantness My friend shows a positive attitude about coping with unpleasantness, pain, or discomfort.	an	s	mo	o	vo
5. Being persevering My friend finishes what is started.	an	s	mo	o	vo
6. Being fair My friend gives equal consideration to the needs of self and others.	an	s	mo	o	vo
7. Being neat My friend behaves in neat and orderly ways.	an	s	mo	o	vo
8. Being reliable My friend consistently fulfills his or her commitments.	an	s	mo	o	vo
9. Being genuine in behavior My friend's behavior is natural and sincere.	an	s	mo	o	vo

Integrity (cont.)	almost never	sometimes	moderately often	often	very often
10. *Accepting blame when at fault* My friend undefensively recognizes and accepts responsibility for his or her own misconduct.	an	s	mo	o	vo
11. *Respecting property rights of others* My friend deals in respectful ways with the personal property rights of others.	an	s	mo	o	vo
12. *Willingly sharing in the work* My friend willingly carries his or her share of the work load.	an	s	mo	o	vo

Number of Low Integrity Scores _____

EMOTIONAL MATURITY RATING FORM

Instructions: Rate your partner/lover/spouse on each of these sixty-three behavioral traits in terms of how often his behavior is observed by you, almost never (*an*); sometimes (*s*); moderately often (*mo*); often (*o*); very often (*vo*). When possible, rate this person's behavior when with you or relating to you. Every item must be rated. Circle the letter code which most accurately describes your partner's behavior. If you do not understand the statement, circle *mo*. Add up the number of ratings that you circled on the left-hand side of the stripe. These low scores should be totaled in each of the four major areas of maturity. Enter these scores on the lines below. Each of these low ratings show a probable area of immaturity.

Date_____ Rater_____
Maturity Scores_____ Partner_____
Number of Low Awareness Scores   _____
Number of Low Relating Scores   _____
Number of Low Competence Scores   _____
Number of Low Integrity Scores   _____

Awareness	almost never	sometimes	moderately often	often	very often
1. *Knowing your own feelings* My friend is aware of and able to report his or her own feelings with accuracy.	an	s	mo	o	vo
2. *Knowing the feelings of others* My friend is sensitive to and can accurately describe the feelings other people have.	an	s	mo	o	vo
3. *Being spontaneously expressive* My friend is emotionally expressive in a natural and immediate way.	an	s	mo	o	vo
4. *Ability to discuss personal feelings* My friend is able to discuss personal feelings with accuracy and is willing to do so.	an	s	mo	o	vo

	almost never	sometimes	moderately often	often	very often

Awareness (cont.)

5. *Coping with mixed feelings*
   My friend accepts the inevitability of having mixed feelings and copes effectively with them.

   | an | s | mo | o | vo |

6. *Curiosity*
   My friend's behavior is inquisitive and investigative.

   | an | s | mo | o | vo |

7. *Getting desires met constructively*
   My friend's personal desires and needs are met in constructive ways.

   | an | s | mo | o | vo |

8. *Coping with fear*
   My friend is aware of his or her fearful feelings, but copes with the situation in effective ways.

   | an | s | mo | o | vo |

9. *Coping with anger*
   My friend is aware of his or her feelings of anger, but copes with the situation in effective ways.

   | an | s | mo | o | vo |

10. *Accepting responsibility for failure*
    My friend undefensively recognizes and accepts his or her own limitations when they are the cause of failure.

    | an | s | mo | o | vo |

Awareness (cont.)

	almost never	sometimes	moderately often	often	very often
11. Coping with frustration and discouragement My friend is positive, persistent, and effective in resolving feelings of frustration and discouragement.	an	s	mo	o	vo
12. Accepting and approving of self My friend freely acknowledges personal limitations and still feels acceptable and worthy	an	s	mo	o	vo
13. Coping with uncertainty My friend accepts some degree of uncertainty as inevitable and retains a positive and willing attitude about dealing with it.	an	s	mo	o	vo
14. Sorting out real and make-believe My friend readily distinguishes reality, knowing clearly the difference between the real and make-believe.	an	s	mo	o	vo

	almost never	sometimes	moderately often	often	very often

Awareness (cont.)

15. *Using imagination constructively*
My friend displays a well-developed imagination and applies these ideas in constructive ways.

	almost never	sometimes	moderately often	often	very often
	an	s	mo	o	vo

Number of Low Awareness Scores _____

Relating

1. *Caring about others*
My friend is sensitive and constructively responsive to the needs of others.

	an	s	mo	o	vo

2. *Getting attention constructively*
My friend gets his or her needs for attention met in constructive ways.

	an	s	mo	o	vo

3. *Earning acceptance*
My friend wins acceptance and inclusion by respecting the values of others.

	an	s	mo	o	vo

4. *Earning approval from others*
My friend earns recognition and praise from others.

	an	s	mo	o	vo

Relating (cont.)

	almost never	sometimes	moderately often	often	very often
5. *Giving affectionate regard* My friend demonstrates warm personal interest in other people.	an	s	mo	o	vo
6. *Being socially responsible* My friend understands his or her ability to affect people for better or for worse and uses this power responsibly.	an	s	mo	o	vo
7. *Being considerate* My friend is aware of other people's feelings and deals with them in considerate ways.	an	s	mo	o	vo
8. *Making friends* My friend makes friends easily and keeps them.	an	s	mo	o	vo
9. *Coping with peer pressure* My friend is able to resist negative peer pressure.	an	s	mo	o	vo
10. *Expressing dissatisfaction constructively* My friend is able to express complaints or criticism in ways that are supportive of the other person.	an	s	mo	o	vo

Relating (cont.)

	almost never	sometimes	moderately often	often	very often
11. *Reciprocating good treatment* My friend recognizes, appreciates, and voluntarily reciprocates good treatment.	an	s	mo	o	vo
12. *Sharing in decision making* My friend lives by the value of obtaining and giving others an equal voice in the decision-making process.	an	s	mo	o	vo
13. *Keeping promises* My friend keeps his or her promises.	an	s	mo	o	vo
14. *Resolving conflicts constructively* My friend, without sacrificing his or her own rights, uses peaceful and constructive means for resolving conflicts.	an	s	mo	o	vo
15. *Willingness to share* My friend willingly shares recognition and possessions.	an	s	mo	o	vo
16. *Becoming more likable* My friend appreciates and constructively uses criticism in order to become a more likable person.	an	s	mo	o	vo

Relating (cont.)

	almost never	sometimes	moderately often	often	very often
17. *Coping with mixed feelings toward people* My friend recognizes, accepts, and deals constructively in disappointments and disagreements with other people.	an	s	mo	o	vo
18. *Responding well to opposite sex* My friend is equally courteous to members of both sexes.	an	s	mo	o	vo

Number of Low Relating Scores _____

Competence

	almost never	sometimes	moderately often	often	very often
1. *Applying energy and effort* My friend is willing to apply energy and effort.	an	s	mo	o	vo
2. *Using knowledge and skills* My friend demonstrates that he or she has acquired knowledge and skills.	an	s	mo	o	vo
3. *Being planful* My friend behaves in planful and organized ways.	an	s	mo	o	vo

Competence (cont.)	almost never	sometimes	moderately often	often	very often
4. *Showing initiative* My friend initiates and implements ideas and projects.	an	s	mo	o	vo
5. *Showing creativity* My friend demonstrates original and inventive ways of doing things.	an	s	mo	o	vo
6. *Behaving with realistic expectations* My friend's expectations and goals are realistic.	an	s	mo	o	vo
7. *Showing self-reliance* My friend relies upon his or her own resources to meet objectives.	an	s	mo	o	vo
8. *Willingly takes on challenge* My friend is willing and eager to try his or her abilities with new tasks.	an	s	mo	o	vo
9. *Showing appropriate caution* My friend anticipates and avoids serious dangers.	an	s	mo	o	vo
10. *Showing self-confidence* My friend shows an attitude of assurance when coping with new situations.	an	s	mo	o	vo
11. *Being responsible* My friend, without being reminded, fulfills obligations.	an	s	mo	o	vo

Competence (cont.)

	almost never	sometimes	moderately often	often	very often
12. *Being motivated to succeed* My friend shows interest in and motivation for success.	an	s	mo	o	vo
13. *Being goal-directed* My friend has highly defined goals that are pursued constructively.	an	s	mo	o	vo
14. *Showing high standards* My friend values and pursues high levels of accuracy and skill in his or her work.	an	s	mo	o	vo
15. *Being cooperative* My friend combines his or her talents well with those of others to achieve a common benefit.	an	s	mo	o	vo
16. *Showing flexibility* My friend is willing to consider new information and try new ways under changing circumstances in order to pursue the same original goal.	an	s	mo	o	vo
17. *Developing personal interests* My friend has strong personal interests and pursues them.	an	s	mo	o	vo

	almost never	sometimes	moderately often	often	very often

Competence (cont.)

18. *Solving problems effectively*
My friend is organized and effective in his or her problem-solving methods.

	an	s	mo	o	vo

Number of Low Competence Scores _____

Integrity

1. *Showing self-control*
My friend's controls prevail over impulse.

	an	s	mo	o	vo

2. *Waiting willingly*
My friend waits with a realistic and calm attitude.

	an	s	mo	o	vo

3. *Being truthful in statements*
My friend is natural, spontaneous, and sincere when describing events.

	an	s	mo	o	vo

4. *Coping with unpleasantness*
My friend shows a positive attitude about coping with unpleasantness, pain, or discomfort.

	an	s	mo	o	vo

5. *Being persevering*
My friend finishes what is started.

	an	s	mo	o	vo

Integrity (cont.)

	almost never	sometimes	moderately often	often	very often
6. *Being fair* My friend gives equal consideration to the needs of self and others.	an	s	mo	o	vo
7. *Being neat* My friend behaves in neat and orderly ways.	an	s	mo	o	vo
8. *Being reliable* My friend consistently fulfills his or her commitments.	an	s	mo	o	vo
9. *Being genuine in behavior* My friend's behavior is natural and sincere.	an	s	mo	o	vo
10. *Accepting blame when at fault* My friend undefensively recognizes and accepts responsibility for his or her own misconduct.	an	s	mo	o	vo
11. *Respecting property rights of others* My friend deals in respectful ways with the personal property rights of others.	an	s	mo	o	vo
12. *Willingly sharing in the work* My friend willingly carries his or her share of the work load.	an	s	mo	o	vo

Number of Low Integrity Scores _____

How to Interpret Your Scores

The Emotional Maturity Rating Form measures the emotional maturity of your partner through your own eyes. It should be kept in mind that a person may respond in a mature fashion in one situation or setting and an immature fashion in a different situation or setting. Likewise, a person may behave maturely with one person and immaturely with another person. We all tend to behave differently in church than we do at a party.

In this part of The Love Test, you are rating your partner's behavior as he or she relates to *you* in your customary shared environment.

Emotional maturity refers in the most general way to those behavioral patterns that make for a good adjustment in life. This requires reasonably good functioning in the four major areas of emotional maturity: awareness, relating, competence, and integrity.

The *awareness* ratings show the extent to which your partner gives behavioral evidence that he or she is an aware person. This means being aware of internal and external environment, being openly honest and receptive in regard to his or her own and other people's feelings, having insight into his or her own motivation, and acting nondefensively and realistically.

Relating indicates how well a person goes about getting his or her social needs met and to what extent that person is respectful and caring about other people.

The *competence* ratings show the extent to which a person is assertive, organized, motivated, flexible, and good at problem solving.

There are two kinds of *integrity* traits: those that show a person's self-discipline (for example, showing self-control and coping with unpleasantness) and those of an ethical nature (for example, being truthful and accepting blame). Together, these two sets of traits reveal a person's character, the extent to which that person can be trusted.

When you have completed the form, add up the number of ratings that you circled on the left-hand side of the stripe. These scores are low and should be totaled in each of the four major areas of emotional maturity. Almost every person has some weaknesses in his or her overall emotional maturity, and these low scores will pinpoint those areas of less strength in the mature person.

For most practical purposes, the difference between mature and immature can be determined by the *one-third* rule. Immaturity is reflected by one-third or more of the scores on the EMRF being low. If your total low scores equal 21, an overall immaturity is indicated. An emotional immaturity in one or more of the four major areas of awareness, relating, competence, or integrity is likewise indicated by the one-third or more rule of thumb.

When you have completed the form, add the number of times you indicated a score of almost never (*an*) or sometimes (*s*). These scores should be added up separately in the four different areas and recorded on your Personal Love Profile (p. 102).

Five or more low awareness scores merit serious attention. A person with this score is immature and not very aware of what he or she is doing. There is a significant lack of insight here.

Six or more low relating scores mean that this person is relatively immature in the ways he or she goes about getting his or her social needs met. This person is not dealing constructively with other people.

Six or more low competence scores show immaturity in being able to get one's needs met constructively. This person is not likely to be effective at work or in solving general life problems.

Four or more low integrity scores show immaturity in either self-discipline or ethical standards.

I Like You; I Love You;
Both of the Above

After reading the first three chapters, it should no longer be confusing to you when you or your partner, one of your friends, or relatives says, "I love you, but I don't like you." You now know that what is being said really means, "I'm romantically excited about you, but you are dishing out emotionally immature treatment."

You now also understand the reverse, when one person tells the other, "I like you, but I don't love you." Then we are describing low romantic interest, and even though there is liking, respect, and trust, there is still that vague empty feeling that is caused by missing romance.

Before you proclaim that you are an expert at diagnosing the love relationship and are ready to determine with authority what the strong and weak points are in your relationship or in those of your friends and relatives, let's move on to the next chapter. This will give you the chance to analyze your own love relationship and compare it with some famous romantic relationships from the worlds of literature and history.

Chapter Four

♡　♡　♡

Romantic
Relationships

Your Romantic Relationship

Now that you and your partner have answered the
Romantic Attraction Questionnaire and have used the
Emotional Maturity Rating Form, you can fill in your
Personal Love Profile. Before you do so, however, read
the sample that follows and shows you where to place the
RAQ and EMRF scores and gives you a key for identifying your kind of love relationship. Then fill in your and
your partner's scores on the blank Personal Love Profile
provided. Once you have discovered your love type,
you can turn to the Love Relationships Chart (p. 101) to
learn more about your relationship. The Romantic Attraction Questionnaire, the Emotional Maturity Rating
Form, Personal Love Profile, and Love Relationships
Chart are the tools to discover your own personal type
of love relationship.

TYPES OF
LOVE RELATIONSHIPS

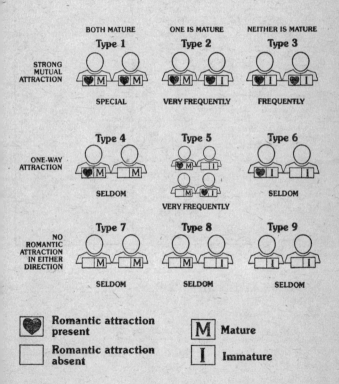

PERSONAL LOVE PROFILE

Number of Low Scores on
Emotional Maturity Rating
Form (EMRF)

Romantic Attraction
Questionnaire (RAQ) Score

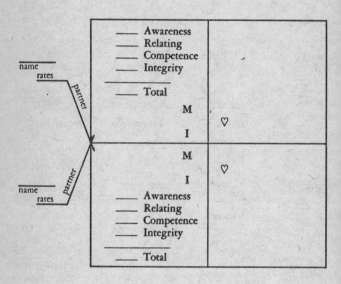

LOVE RELATIONSHIP TYPE_____

Number of low EMRF Scores
0–20 low scores total   M
21 or more low scores total   I

RAQ Scores
♥ 220–300 strong attraction
♥ 200–220 borderline
♡ 180–200 weak attraction

Types of Love Relationships

Type 1 ♥ M ♥ M	Type 4 ♥ M ♡ M	Type 7 ♡ M ♡ M
Type 2 ♥ M ♥ I	[Type 5 ♥ M ♡ I / Type 5 ♡ M ♥ I]	Type 8 ♡ M ♡ I
Type 3 ♥ I ♥ I	Type 6 ♥ I ♡ I	Type 9 ♡ I ♡ I

PERSONAL LOVE PROFILE

Number of Low Scores on Emotional Maturity Rating Form (EMRF)	Romantic Attraction Questionnaire (RAQ) Score

	John rates Mary on her emotional maturity, using the Emotional Maturity Rating Form on pp. 74–85 M	Mary rates her feelings about John, using the Romantic Attraction Questionnaire on pp. 45–49.
MARY name rates *partner*	John circles letter to indicate score I	♡ Mary indicates score
JOHN name rates *partner*	Mary circles letter to indicate score M I	♡ John indicates score
	Mary rates John on his emotional maturity, using the Emotional Maturity Rating Form on pp. 85–96.	John rates his feelings about Mary, using the Romantic Attraction Questionnaire on pp. 49–53.

LOVE RELATIONSHIP TYPE_____

Number of low EMRF Scores
0–20 low scores total   M
21 or more low scores total   I

RAQ Scores
♥ 220–300 strong attraction
❦ 200–220 borderline
♡ 180–200 weak attraction

Types of Love Relationships

Type 1 ♥ M ♥ M	Type 4 ♥ M ♡ M	Type 7 ♡ M ♡ M
Type 2 ♥ M ♥ I	⎡ Type 5 ♥ M ♡ I ⎤ ⎣ Type 5 ♡ M ♥ I ⎦	Type 8 ♡ M ♡ I
Type 3 ♥ I ♥ I	Type 6 ♥ I ♡ I	Type 9 ♡ I ♡ I

Famous Romantic Relationships

After working with these materials as long as I have, I have come to view *every* romance vis-à-vis these rating scales, even when I am watching a movie or television. So I have put together a few special case histories that I hope will give you a good look at exactly how the RAQ and the EMRF work together.

Love makes the world go around, and there are all kinds of love matches and all kinds of lovers. Some surmount all odds to work out their relationships. For them, love conquers all. Some turn to drink when the going gets tough; sometimes the tough get going; some love one but turn to another for comfort and caring. There are men who fight wars for the love of a woman. There are women who will do anything to get their man's attention. There are men who are blind to love until one day they seem to see as if for the first time. Suddenly their feelings come into focus and they realize the importance of love in their lives.

Now let's get some practice at mastering this method of understanding the love relationship by looking at how the Personal Love Profiles of some famous romantic couples would probably appear.

Jane Nearly Had a Calamity and Bill Went Wild When He Found Out

Wild Bill Hickok and Calamity Jane were wild about each other. They just didn't show it. Jane knew she loved Bill, but she was so discouraged by the way he treated her that she acted like she didn't care about him. She was too proud to show her feelings.

Meanwhile, Wild Bill kept treating Jane like a kid sister. He liked, respected, and trusted her, but he just didn't recognize his romantic feelings for her. He suffered from a mild fear problem. He was afraid that showing his true feelings would make him less of a man, or

PERSONAL LOVE PROFILE

Number of Low Scores on
Emotional Maturity Rating
Form (EMRF)

Romantic Attraction
Questionnaire (RAQ) Score

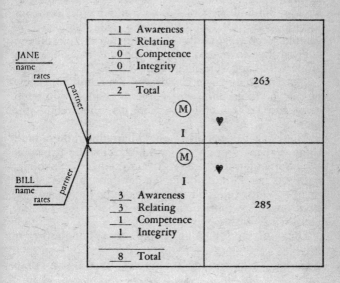

LOVE RELATIONSHIP TYPE_____1_____

Number of low EMRF Scores

0–20 low scores total   M
21 or more low scores total   I

RAQ Scores

♥ 220–300 strong attraction
♥ 200–220 borderline
♡ 180–200 weak attraction

Types of Love Relationships

Type 1 ♥ M ♥ M	Type 4 ♥ M ♡ M	Type 7 ♡ M ♡ M
Type 2 ♥ M ♥ I	⎡Type 5 ♥ M ♡ I⎤	Type 8 ♡ M ♡ I
	⎣Type 5 ♡ M ♥ I⎦	
Type 3 ♥ I ♥ I	Type 6 ♥ I ♡ I	Type 9 ♡ I ♡ I

would take away from the energy and time he needed for his own pursuits.

Jane would do anything to get Bill to notice her as a woman, but she knew that you can't get a man with a gun. That would be a calamity.

The couple spent a lot of time together and had several mutual interests. Jane could ride and shoot as well as Bill and they offered each other great companionship. But Bill just didn't treat Jane the way she wanted to be treated. And he never did come right out and ask her to marry him, so she was stuck hanging around, fretting, and feeling miserable.

Then one day Indians captured Jane, and Bill knew he had to rescue her or die trying. His fears dropped away and he was able to unveil his true feelings for Jane.

The Love Test materials would have found them both to be very mature, and to have high romantic attraction for each other. Bill suffered from being too involved with his work, and their relationship suffered from neglect. Once Bill realized how much he loved Jane, he gave her the attention that showed her value to him, and they lived happier ever after.

Diagnosis: A Type-One couple almost gone astray.

Scarlett's Chance for True Love Was Gone With the Wind

Scarlett O'Hara lead a sheltered life in prewar Georgia, where little was expected of her. Her mother and her servants waited on her hand and foot, and her uncommon beauty made each beau her slave. Her life-style left little room for maturity, and when she was sixteen she decided she was in love with her neighbor, Ashley. Ashley was infatuated with Scarlett, but was mature enough to know that any relationship with her would never work out. So he married his cousin Melanie, who loved him very much.

Scarlett's immaturity led her from romantic disaster to romantic disaster. First she married Ashley's cousin.

PERSONAL LOVE PROFILE

Number of Low Scores on
Emotional Maturity Rating
Form (EMRF)

Romantic Attraction
Questionnaire (RAQ) Score

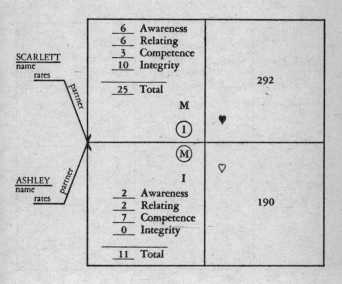

LOVE RELATIONSHIP TYPE _____ 5 _____

Number of low EMRF Scores
0–20 low scores total   M
21 or more low scores total   I

RAQ Scores
♥ 220–300 strong attraction
♥ 200–220 borderline
♡ 180–200 weak attraction

Types of Love Relationships

Type 1 ♥ M ♥ M	Type 4 ♥ M ♡ M	Type 7 ♡ M ♡ M
Type 2 ♥ M ♥ I	⎡ Type 5 ♥ M ♡ I ⎤	Type 8 ♡ M ♡ I
Type 3 ♥ I ♥ I	⎣ Type 5 ♥ M ♥ I ⎦	Type 9 ♡ I ♡ I

PERSONAL LOVE PROFILE

Number of Low Scores on
Emotional Maturity Rating
Form (EMRF)

Romantic Attraction
Questionnaire (RAQ) Score

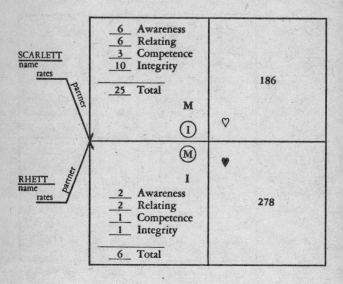

SCARLETT
name
rates

partner

6	Awareness
6	Relating
3	Competence
10	Integrity
25	Total

M

Ⓘ

186   ♡

Ⓜ

I

♥   278

RHETT
name
rates

partner

2	Awareness
2	Relating
1	Competence
1	Integrity
6	Total

LOVE RELATIONSHIP TYPE_____5_____

Number of low EMRF Scores
0–20 low scores total   M
21 or more low scores total   I

RAQ Scores
♥ 220–300 strong attraction
♥ 200–220 borderline
♡ 180–200 weak attraction

Types of Love Relationships

Type 1 ♥ M ♥ M	Type 4 ♥ M ♡ M	Type 7 ♡ M ♡ M
Type 2 ♥ M ♥ I	[Type 5 ♥ M ♡ I	Type 8 ♡ M ♡ I
Type 3 ♥ I ♥ I	Type 5 ♡ M ♥ I]	Type 9 ♡ I ♡ I
	Type 6 ♥ I ♡ I	

Then she married her sister's boyfriend. Finally she married Rhett Butler, although she made it clear to him that she didn't love him. Rhett didn't mind; his RAQ for Scarlett was so high that he was sure he could make her love him. He knew Scarlett suffered from a fear of closeness (see p. 178) and felt that she could be reconditioned to trust and love after she outgrew the traumas of the war that brought them together. Scarlett was used to marrying men for her convenience rather than for true love, so she and Rhett were married.

She continued to pine for Ashley and to try to manipulate him into loving her. Her immaturity affected every relationship she was involved in and finally drove her husband to desperate behavior. When disaster and death entered their lives, they had no way to communicate with each other.

Rhett began drinking. Scarlett's immature behavior continued to be abrasive. Rhett was consumed with love for her but knew that her heart was with another man. Finally, he left her.

When a maturing experience made Scarlett see that her love for Ashley had been a fantasy, she tried to get Rhett to stay with her and give her one more chance. Rhett had been so hurt over the years that, finally, he just didn't give a damn.

Diagnosis: Two classic Type-Five relationships.

Guenevere and Arthur and Lancelot Went Around and Around and Around

Art knew that his parents would pick his bride for him, so he never worried too much about true love. He was mature enough to know his duty to his family, his country, and his kingdom. He was matched with the fair Gwen and, although he wondered before the wedding what she would be like, he was the type of man who would do his best to love her. When she did arrive in Camelot, he was delighted and surprised to find himself immediately attracted to her.

PERSONAL LOVE PROFILE

Number of Low Scores on
Emotional Maturity Rating
Form (EMRF)

Romantic Attraction
Questionnaire (RAQ) Score

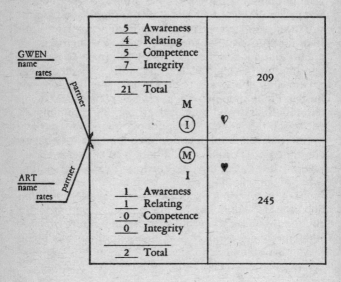

LOVE RELATIONSHIP TYPE _____ Borderline 2/5

Number of low EMRF Scores
0–20 low scores total   M
21 or more low scores total   I

RAQ Scores
♥ 220–300 strong attraction
♥ 200–220 borderline
♡ 180–200 weak attraction

Types of Love Relationships

Type 1 ♥ M ♥ M	Type 4 ♥ M ♡ M	Type 7 ♡ M ♡ M
Type 2 ♥ M ♥ I	[Type 5 ♥ M ♡ I]	Type 8 ♡ M ♡ I
Type 3 ♥ I ♥ I	[Type 5 ♡ M ♥ I]	Type 9 ♡ I ♡ I
	Type 6 ♥ I ♥ I	

PERSONAL LOVE PROFILE

Number of Low Scores on
Emotional Maturity Rating
Form (EMRF)

Romantic Attraction
Questionnaire (RAQ) Score

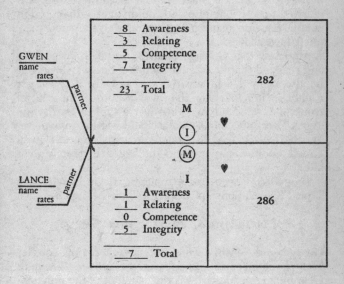

LANCE
name
rates

GWEN
name
rates

partner

8 Awareness		
3 Relating		
5 Competence		
7 Integrity		
23 Total		282
M		
(I)	♥	
(M)	♥	
I		
1 Awareness		
1 Relating		
0 Competence		286
5 Integrity		
7 Total		

LOVE RELATIONSHIP TYPE_____2_____

Number of low EMRF Scores
0–20 low scores total M
21 or more low scores total I

RAQ Scores
♥ 220–300 strong attraction
♥ 200–220 borderline
♡ 180–200 weak attraction

Types of Love Relationships

Type 1 ♥ M ♥ M   Type 4 ♥ M ♡ M   Type 7 ♡ M ♡ M

Type 2 ♥ M ♥ I   ⌈Type 5 ♥ M ♡ I⌉   Type 8 ♡ M ♡ I
                   ⌊Type 5 ♡ M ♥ I⌋

Type 3 ♥ I ♥ I   Type 6 ♥ I ♡ I   Type 9 ♡ I ♡ I

They married and expected to live happily ever after. Gwen was borderline in her feelings for Art—she wasn't passionately in love with him—but she married him because she was told to and she was not unhappy with their relationship. She met Lance, one of the knights of her husband's court. The mutual romantic attraction between them was intense. But because Gwen was married to someone else and couldn't get a divorce, the couple ran into many difficulties as they pursued their illicit love affair.

Art knew that Gwen was having an affair with Lance and realized that he was the victim of one-way love, but he also knew that he was the king and that if Gwen got caught in her loveplay, they would both be in a lot of trouble. Gwen and Art were just a typical Borderline Types Two/Five couple—an accident waiting to happen. When the accident happened, it wasn't pretty. Gwen ended up in a convent and did *not* live happily ever after.

Diagnosis: Gwen was a romantic virgin caught in a Type-Five relationship, having a Type-Two affair.

Who's Afraid? Martha and George

George and Martha were not a very happy couple. They lived near the campus at the university where George taught. Martha was the daughter of the university president. It's hard to know their true story, because each person tells the facts in a manner devised to hurt the other. While they have moments of happiness together, most of the time they fight. Martha reminds George that he is a nobody and that he owes his tenure at the university to her father. George confronts Martha with the terrible truth that she has been lying about their having a son. They both drink to excess. Martha likes to tell George she can drink him under the table.

Diagnosis: A classic Type-Three couple.

Their RAQ scores are mutually high. With effective therapy, George and Martha would have made a go of it. It would have been long, arduous therapy for them

PERSONAL LOVE PROFILE

Number of Low Scores on
Emotional Maturity Rating
Form (EMRF)

Romantic Attraction
Questionnaire (RAQ) Score

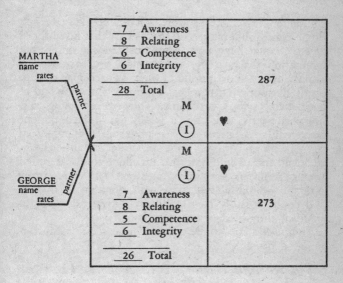

MARTHA
name
rates

partner

7 Awareness	
8 Relating	
6 Competence	
6 Integrity	
28 Total	287

M

Ⓘ ♥

GEORGE
name
rates

partner

M

Ⓘ ♥

7 Awareness	
8 Relating	
5 Competence	
6 Integrity	
26 Total	273

LOVE RELATIONSHIP TYPE _____ 3 _____

Number of low EMRF Scores
0–20 low scores total   M
21 or more low scores total   I

RAQ Scores
♥ 220–300 strong attraction
♥ 200–220 borderline
♡ 180–200 weak attraction

Types of Love Relationships

Type 1 ♥ M ♥ M	Type 4 ♥ M ♡ M	Type 7 ♡ M ♡ M
Type 2 ♥ M ♥ I	⎡Type 5 ♥ M ♡ I⎤	Type 8 ♡ M ♡ I
	⎣Type 5 ♡ M ♥ I⎦	
Type 3 ♥ I ♥ I	Type 6 ♥ I ♡ I	Type 9 ♡ I ♡ I

as individuals and as a couple, but because of the high degree of romantic attraction they shared, it would have been worth it.

For Romeo and Juliet, Parting Is Such Self-defeating Sorrow

Although their families were not on speaking terms, Romeo and Juliet happened to meet and fall instantly in love. It could have been a case of one-way or mutual infatuation because the relationship progressed very rapidly over a short period of time, as each managed to evade disapproving families and unite. But they had at least two serious problems: They were young and inexperienced, and Juliet's family hired incompetent nursemaids. As a result, a relationship that might in time have proved to be genuine mutual romantic chemistry and thus would have had excellent potential ended tragically in an immature manner. With time, they probably would have become more emotionally mature and could possibly have had a Type-One relationship. Instead, they died before their time.

Diagnosis: Potentially a Type-Three relationship terminated prematurely.

Cleopatra and Caesar, Then Antony, Then the Asp—and That's Where It All Ends

Cleo was young, but she was cunning, ambitious, and not anxious to lose control of her life or her country. She had already beaten her brother out for the throne and was not about to be daunted by Caesar. When Caesar conquered her country, she rolled herself up in a carpet and had herself delivered to his feet. He fell in love with her and proclaimed her queen of the Nile.

They had a wild and passionate love affair, although Cleo was acting her part to keep her throne and power intact. The match might have lasted forever, or as long as Caesar stayed in power, except that theirs was a

PERSONAL LOVE PROFILE

Number of Low Scores on
Emotional Maturity Rating
Form (EMRF)

Romantic Attraction
Questionnaire (RAQ) Score

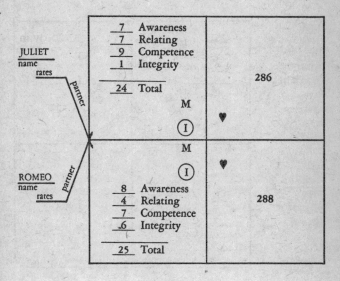

LOVE RELATIONSHIP TYPE _____ 3 _____

Number of low EMRF Scores
0–20 low scores total   M
21 or more low scores total   I

RAQ Scores
♥ 220–300 strong attraction
♥ 200–220 borderline
♡ 180–200 weak attraction

Types of Love Relationships

Type 1 ♥ M ♥ M   Type 4 ♥ M ♡ M   Type 7 ♡ M ♡ M

Type 2 ♥ M ♥ I   [Type 5 ♥ M ♡ I]   Type 8 ♡ M ♡ I
                              [Type 5 ♡ M ♥ I]

Type 3 ♥ I ♥ I   Type 6 ♥ I ♡ I   Type 9 ♡ I ♡ I

PERSONAL LOVE PROFILE

Number of Low Scores on
Emotional Maturity Rating
Form (EMRF)

Romantic Attraction
Questionnaire (RAQ) Score

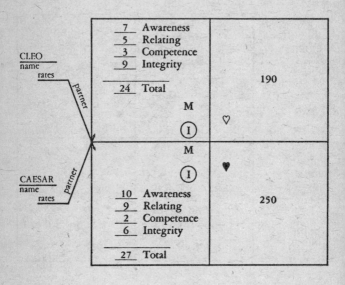

CLEO
name
rates

_7_ Awareness
_5_ Relating
_3_ Competence
_9_ Integrity

_24_ Total

M

Ⓘ

190

♡

M

Ⓘ

♥

CAESAR
name
rates

_10_ Awareness
_9_ Relating
_2_ Competence
_6_ Integrity

_27_ Total

250

LOVE RELATIONSHIP TYPE_____6_____

Number of low EMRF Scores
0–20 low scores total   M
21 or more low scores total   I

RAQ Scores
♥ 220–300 strong attraction
♥ 200–220 borderline
♡ 180–200 weak attraction

Types of Love Relationships

Type 1 ♥ M ♥ M	Type 4 ♥ M ♡ M	Type 7 ♡ M ♡ M
Type 2 ♥ M ♥ I	[Type 5 ♥ M ♡ I / Type 5 ♡ M ♥ I]	Type 8 ♡ M ♡ I
Type 3 ♥ I ♥ I	Type 6 ♥ I ♡ I	Type 9 ♡ I ♡ I

PERSONAL LOVE PROFILE

Number of Low Scores on
Emotional Maturity Rating
Form (EMRF)

Romantic Attraction
Questionnaire (RAQ) Score

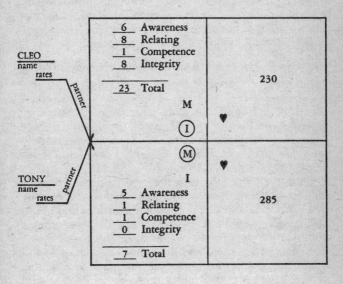

CLEO
name
rates
partner

6	Awareness
8	Relating
1	Competence
8	Integrity
23	Total

M

Ⓘ

♥

230

Ⓜ

I

TONY
name
rates
partner

♥

285

5	Awareness
1	Relating
1	Competence
0	Integrity
7	Total

LOVE RELATIONSHIP TYPE _____2_____

Number of low EMRF Scores

0–20 low scores total   M
21 or more low scores total   I

RAQ Scores

♥ 220–300 strong attraction
♥ 200–220 borderline
♡ 180–200 weak attraction

Types of Love Relationships

Type 1 ♥ M ♥ M	Type 4 ♥ M ♡ M	Type 7 ♡ M ♡ M
Type 2 ♥ M ♥ I	[Type 5 ♥ M ♡ I] [Type 5 ♡ M ♥ I]	Type 8 ♡ M ♡ I
Type 3 ♥ I ♥ I	Type 6 ♥ I ♡ I	Type 9 ♡ I ♡ I

typical Type-Six relationship—another accident waiting to happen.

When Caesar sent Tony to keep an eye on things in Egypt, the accident happened. Cleo and Tony fell madly in love. Tony had a higher RAQ for Cleo and became blinded by his interest in her. And Cleo knew just how to manipulate Tony. Although Tony was mature in most ways, he was a great vacillator. Cleo got him in a lot of hot water.

Diagnosis: A typical Type-Two relationship.

Lucy Just Couldn't Accept That Schroeder Never Cared Peanuts for Her

It's double trouble for Lucy and Schroeder, a very typical Type-Five couple. Lucy is highly attracted to Schroeder, but, alas, it's one-way love. Schroeder only rates Lucy at a dismal 90. He barely knows she's alive. Then, to make matters worse, Lucy has a severe maturity problem. She falls into the typical triple-whammy pattern of being demanding, critical, and angry. She definitely needs to find out if the doctor is in and to see him on a regular basis. Then perhaps she can increase her maturity so she can see that, for the past twenty-five years or so, she's been in love with a man who will never notice her. Then she can move on to someone else. Perhaps she will find a nice red-haired boy who cares for her, and if she grows up emotionally—it could work out.

Diagnosis: Type-Five relationship.

Famous case histories were based on the following sources:

- Wild Bill Hickok and Calamity Jane: many movies about Calamity Jane.
- Scarlett and Rhett: *Gone with the Wind* by Margaret Mitchell.
- Arthur and Guenevere and Lancelot: *Camelot*, the movie.

PERSONAL LOVE PROFILE

Number of Low Scores on
Emotional Maturity Rating
Form (EMRF)

Romantic Attraction
Questionnaire (RAQ) Score

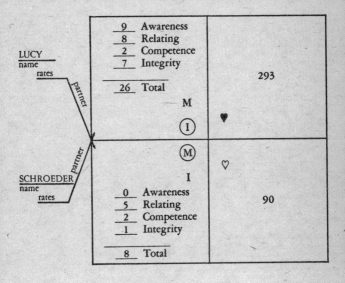

LUCY
name
rates
partner

SCHROEDER
name
rates
partner

9	Awareness
8	Relating
2	Competence
7	Integrity
26	Total

M

Ⓘ

❤

293

Ⓜ

I

♡

0	Awareness
5	Relating
2	Competence
1	Integrity
8	Total

90

LOVE RELATIONSHIP TYPE _____ 5 _____

Number of low EMRF Scores   **RAQ Scores**
0–20 low scores total   M   ❤ 220–300 strong attraction
21 or more low scores total I   ❤ 200–220 borderline
                                    ♡ 180–200 weak attraction

Types of Love Relationships

Type 1 ❤ M ❤ M   Type 4 ❤ M ♡ M   Type 7 ♡ M ♡ M
Type 2 ❤ M ❤ I   Type 5 ❤ M ♡ I   Type 8 ♡ M ♡ I
Type 3 ❤ I ❤ I   [Type 5 ♡ M ❤ I] Type 9 ♡ I ♡ I
                  [Type 6 ❤ I ♡ I]

- George and Martha: *Who's Afraid of Virginia Woolf?* by Edward Albee.
- Romeo and Juliet: *Romeo and Juliet* by William Shakespeare.
- Cleopatra and Caesar and Antony: *Antony and Cleopatra* by William Shakespeare.
- Lucy and Schroeder: *Peanuts* by Charles Schulz.

Chapter Five

♡ ♡ ♡

Building
Mature Love

BOTH ARE MATURE

Together Happily

Everybody loves a lover and that's why I like Type-One couples.

They are mature lovers.

That's not to say that they don't have their problems, that they are immune to their own share of life crises. Being Type One does not automatically mean a couple will not have any problems. But Type Ones have learned to work together and to share the burden of their problems and crises. No problem is so big that they can't survive it—together. As a result, Type Ones rarely come in for therapy. Or, when they do come in, they are having such a silly squabble that as soon as they use The Love Test materials and see the results in black and white, they realize how simply their differences can be worked out.

Jim and Diane were high-school sweethearts. Both tried dating others while they were in college, but they continued to find themselves irresistibly drawn back together. They shared a special sense of excitement that they never experienced with anyone else. They felt that they belonged together. During their senior year in college they married.

After finishing college, Diane got a job and supported Jim while he attended law school. Once established with a law firm, Jim made enough money for Diane to quit working. She spent a year doing charity work, then became pregnant. The couple had two children and Diane stayed home while Jim worked his way up the office ladder of success.

As the children grew up, Diane decided to go back to school. She got a law degree and soon found a job in another law firm. The years while she was going to school and juggling motherhood were difficult and put a strain on the marriage. Diane was overworked, tense, and short on energy. She was trying to be superwoman and the stress showed in her marriage. Jim suggested that she slow down. Diane felt that Jim didn't want her to succeed and that he was jealous that she had also become a lawyer. When Jim and Diane came to me and used The Love Test, they rated each other very highly.

After seventeen years of marriage, Jim and Diane couldn't have been more in love. and they both had a solid amount of emotional maturity. A divorce would have been out of the question, and therapy was not really needed. All they needed to do was remember the basic rules that make for good relationships.

Type-One couples have become Type Ones because they have mastered these techniques. Many Type Ones didn't start off in that category. Most began as Type Twos, with one partner leading the other toward better emotional maturity. They became Type Ones when both realized that a happy marriage doesn't just happen; it's built by persistent, daily devoted attention to each other's needs.

As we've already seen, romantic attraction cannot be created, but once it exists and is accompanied by a high enough emotional maturity, a fulfilling relationship can be achieved. Type Ones practice Bessell's Ten Rules of

PERSONAL LOVE PROFILE

Number of Low Scores on
Emotional Maturity Rating
Form (EMRF)

Romantic Attraction
Questionnaire (RAQ) Score

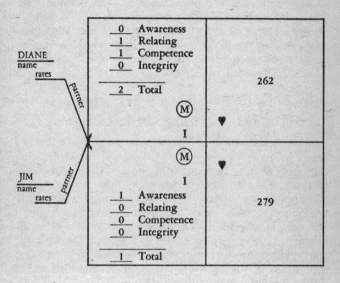

DIANE
_____
name
  rates

partner

0	Awareness	
1	Relating	
1	Competence	262
0	Integrity	
___		
2	Total	

Ⓜ

I

♥

JIM
_____
name
  rates

partner

Ⓜ

I

♥

1	Awareness	
0	Relating	
0	Competence	279
0	Integrity	
___		
1	Total	

LOVE RELATIONSHIP TYPE _____1_____

Number of low EMRF Scores

0–20 low scores total   M
21 or more low scores total   I

RAQ Scores

♥ 220–300 strong attraction
♥ 200–220 borderline
♡ 180–200 weak attraction

Types of Love Relationships

Type 1 ♥ M ♥ M	Type 4 ♥ M ♡ M	Type 7 ♡ M ♡ M
Type 2 ♥ M ♥ I	⌈ Type 5 ♥ M ♡ I ⌉	Type 8 ♡ M ♡ I
	⌊ Type 5 ♡ M ♥ I ⌋	
Type 3 ♥ I ♥ I	Type 6 ♥ I ♡ I	Type 9 ♡ I ♡ I

ᵣness (below) every day, more or less uncon-
. As you begin to practice them, you will see if
you

- Already practicing them as part of your normal daily
  routine without any thought to their uniqueness
  (therefore, you're a true Type One).
- Able to realize the importance of these actions (you
  can become a Type-One couple).
- Not capable of absorbing these rules into your life-
  style; they are just too demanding for you to consider.
  (Low emotional maturity—true love will probably
  elude you until you grow up.)

Bessell's Ten Rules of Togetherness—
The Ten Commandments for an
Emotionally Mature Relationship

The task of fully understanding an individual's pattern
of emotional maturities and immaturities is formidable.
Giving supportive confrontation for each and every
incidence of immaturity is clearly impossible. To help
the couple who want to guide each other to emotional
maturity, I have summarized the most useful guidelines
for building an emotionally mature relationship. Bessell's
Ten Rules of Togetherness can help everyone improve
his or her love relationship.

Rule One: Never Guess/Never Assume

One of the greatest sources of trouble between couples
is guessing. In our dealings with other people we are
constantly making assumptions. Many, make that most,
of these assumptions are wrong. You may imagine that
your partner's silence means anger, disinterest, worry,
pain, fear, or hopeful expectations. There probably is a
different reason for the silence, but because your lover
is mum, you come up with dozens of imagined reasons
for the silence. Then you are up against your own

imagination, your own guesses, and your mistaken assumptions.

It is a sad fact that most guesses are wrong and a wrong guess is almost always wrong in some negative direction. (No one ever guesses that something went "wrong" for a "good" reason.)

So if you want to avoid all this pain, misery, and uncertainty, you can do one simple thing. You can ask. *Develop the habit of asking.* Never guess. Never assume.

Rule Two: Your Partner Is Not a Sex Object

If you want to succeed in your relationship, you must first and foremost see your partner as a human being and a companion, not as a sex object. Sexual roles and lovemaking are only *part* of your relationship.

In the best of relationships, each partner shares common bonds with the other. Ask yourself if you like, trust, and respect your mate. These are the vital elements for making a long-lasting, satisfying relationship. Insisting that your partner fill only a sexual role will only limit and eventually destroy your relationship.

Rule Three: Teamwork Makes Love Work

Togetherness is a very complex thing. While people live together and are married in what is supposed to be a very close relationship, they often operate in totally separate spheres of action. They may be sharing the rent, the same apartment or home, even the same bed and supposedly the same lifetimes, but they aren't really sharing at all. They are only married legally. Nothing about their individual actions marries them to the same time and space.

A great deal of damage is done by unilateral, independent actions. Love works only when the partners work together as a team. Teamwork makes love work. One-way decisions, made *without* the approval of the partner when the partner's life is affected, are poison to a lasting relationship. In a good relationship, people really invest fully. They merge their physical energies and their skills, their social, emotional, and financial resources, and they function as a team.

Rule Four: Give the Four A's Every Day

The four A's that make any successful relationship are:

Attention

Acceptance

Approval

Affection

Demonstrate the four A's in any and every way you can on a regular basis: Show affection, give attention, make your acceptance and approval well known. One-to-one time (see p. 134) provides all of the four A's. As you give your full and serious attention for ten minutes each day to all of your partner's bragging and complaining, you will be giving not only attention, but also acceptance by tuning in to your partner's world of feelings and experience, your approval of them as a person worth having your devoted attention, and you will deliver that exclusive personal interest that implies "at this moment I am reassuring you that you are the most important person in the world to me." One-to-one time is for sharing interests and concerns, so just listen, and try to avoid getting into discussions or problem solving. That should be done at another time.

Attention is everyone's most fundamental need. Giving attention shows interest. Attention is recognition; it shows that you care. Accept your lover as someone special to you—this goes beyond including him or her in your conversations and plans. Give your positive endorsement of your love's personal value. Approve of your lover by reinforcing what he or she does. This assures your partner that you have a good relationship with each other; approval lets your partner know where he or she stands. Affection is the richest kind of endorsement you can give anyone; it is an act of affirmation that says you really care. (Be sure to hug, kiss, and caress your partner often.)

Whatever you choose to do, do it to demonstrate that you care. This doesn't mean giving up your independence; it just means being aware of your partner's needs. Simple recognition is a very basic human need that is all too often ignored. It is one of the main ingredients in a true and lasting love. Everyone wants to get affection; few people think about *giving* it. Attention is soul food and a steady diet will provide good nourishment to your marriage.

Attention is personal notice.

Acceptance is inclusion.

Approval is a pat on the back.

Affection is showing you feel your lover is a special, valuable person.

Rule Five: Build Common Interests

Many couples marry or unite after a whirlwind courtship during which infatuation reigned supreme. Sometime afterward—months, years, decades—they find they have less and less in common and nothing to say to each other.

By the time the couples, or individuals, come to a marriage counselor, they are complaining that they have nothing in common. They are often secretly wondering why they married each other.

For the couple that has reasonably good maturity and feels strong romantic attraction, *there are always things that they can learn to share*. It just takes an open mind and a little curiosity.

The truth is that I find it extremely rare for a couple to separate because of lack of common interests. People split up because of a lack of mutual romantic interest and because of uncaring treatment. If you complain about having nothing in common, perhaps your romantic attraction level is so low that you don't care to have anything in common. Or perhaps you are not taking a personal interest in your partner's inner self.

Rule Six: Learn to Be a Better Lover

Lovers are made, not born. The sooner everyone learns this, the happier all lovers will be.

Very few men are taught how to be considerate and affectionate with women. Very few women know much about pleasing a man until the men in their lives have shown them. Common misconceptions are that men are "born lovers" and women are so naive that their men must teach them everything.

Some men do know without learning what pleases a woman, just as some women know without being told what to do. But these people are few. Everyone else has to *learn*.

Many of us feel cheated and hurt if we don't get the kind of lovemaking we want. The best way to learn loving is to show and tell each other. Sharing is essential and intimate; sharing provides the best education.

Don't be too embarrassed to ask for what pleases you. Your lover is not a mind reader.

Rule Seven: Don't Play Games

Game playing has no constructive role in a good relationship. Fighting and game playing both should be eliminated from your love life. Game playing may entrap your partner, but it will never make for a happy relationship.

Avoid

• Making each other jealous.

• Using the silent treatment.

• Withholding sex.

- Bargaining.
- Keeping score.
- Getting even.
- Proving the other wrong.
- Complaining to outsiders.
- Using in-laws, parents, or children in your struggle.
- One-upmanship with intent to outdo.
- Trying to buy love with gifts.

Rule Eight: Take Risks for More Intimacy

Intimacy often means taking a risk to be close. The very word comes from the Latin root meaning "within." To be truly intimate, you must allow your partner to come within your personal boundaries, and sometimes this hurts. Of course, the rewards of intimacy are so great that it's very much worth the risk, but the risk is there. Occasional rejection won't do you any permanent harm.

Everyone wants to be accepted by his or her lover. Everyone wants to feel that deep down inside, no matter what small mistakes you make, your lover understands you, knows the real you, and sees past whatever your mistakes are, into the real you, the intimate, secret you. But no one can accept you to that degree until he or she gets to meet and appreciate that inner, secret you. And that means going for the gamble; that means leaving yourself open to the person of your choice—so he or she can see all there is to see and then make the judgment to accept you or not.

This requires both courage and forethought. I don't recommend that you open up all at once in one big marathon this-is-the-real-me session. You could scare your lover and yourself needlessly. Practice slowly and steadily revealing yourselves to each other. It takes time to get to know someone so thoroughly that you can offer the kind of acceptance true love assures. But sharing your most private feelings and thoughts builds lasting intimacy, trust, and a happy relationship.

Rule Nine: Be Polite

The opposite side of intimacy is the tendency to feel that, once you know a person so well, you don't have to be polite or courteous. Yet, does it make any sense to be more polite with someone you are not in love with or with someone who is of less value than your lover? Politeness says, "I care about you," and it's more important than a bouquet of flowers, a box of chocolates, or a talking birthday card. Open the door for each other, lean over and unlock the other side of the car, hold the chair for easier sitting, help carry in the groceries. Show affection by being polite.

Rule Ten: Give as Much of Yourself as You Can

This is a very simple but essential commitment. If you give all you can of your time and love to your partner, without questions or expectations, you will be taking care of your partner and yourself. There will be no tug-of-war, no power struggle, few demands, fights, or misunderstandings.

But the giving rule only works when *both* partners realize, recognize, and appreciate what the other partner is doing and then reciprocate by giving as much of himself or herself as possible.

If your partner is truly committed to you and looks out for your well-being before his or her own, you will *spontaneously* get back all the love, caring, and affection you have given.

When emotional maturity and romantic attraction are high, and each partner gives of himself or herself to the other, you will indeed live happier ever after.

Type-One Couples Work at It

Bessell's Ten Rules of Togetherness are practiced daily by couples with Type-One relationships. Couples who aspire to be Type Ones would do well to study these tips and begin incorporating them into their lives.

A Type-One relationship only stays that way with constant nurturing and caring. Sometimes only one partner is nurturing the relationship; almost always the two partners invest differing degrees of emotion into the relationship. For example, Partner One in the diagram that follows is a hundred percent legally married, but is only fifteen percent emotionally invested in the relationship. Partner One continues to lead his life in a unilateral way. So even though legally married, in essence the person is only fifteen percent married. Partner Two is also a hundred percent legally married, but is eighty percent emotionally invested in the relationship. This person is ready, willing, and able to

Degrees of Emotional Investment in a Relationship

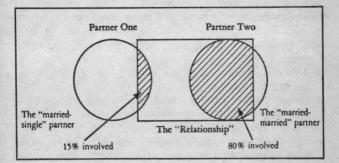

Two partners may invest very different degrees of emotional involvement in their relationship. Both partners must be adequately invested to make a relationship successful.

have a true partnership. Both partners must make an adequate emotional investment in the relationship before that relationship can be meaningful and satisfying.

Some couples know that a relationship has to be built; they work on it and bring out the best in each other. In time, the relationship steadily improves.

Unfortunately, many couples assume that the relationship is already established at the outset. These couples expect to be taken care of and don't make the necessary efforts to improve their relationship. Typically, they grow to resent each other more and more, and invest less and less in the relationship. In the end, one pushes for a divorce, or if they remain together, it is in a state of mutual bitterness, held together by mutual morbid dependency.

Rx for Type-One Relationships

Type-One lovers are only in a Type-One relationship because they work at making the most of what they have. It is not unusual for a Type-One relationship to suffer from neglect and become a Type One gone astray. When this happens, a couple can quickly get back on the right track by following a few simple steps:

- Give daily attention, acceptance, approval, and affection.
- Discuss issues and share equally in the decision-making process.
- Invest twenty minutes each day in one-to-one time (see p. 134), listening without interruption to each other's bragging and complaining.
- Ask your lover what he or she needs, then do your best to give it.

Your Emotional Maturity—Strengths and Weaknesses

Now that you have to tools to help each other gain greater emotional maturity, let's explore the behavioral traits that make up mature behavior. As you read this section, refer to your own and your partner's EMRF, pinpoint your areas of greatest strength and weakness. Then, together, make a plan to help each other and your relationship.

I ask all the couples who come to me for help to issue each other a "license to confront." That way both partners are more willing to give *and* receive supportive confrontation. The examples given throughout this discussion of the behavioral traits of emotional maturity will help you learn some of the tricks of the trade for using supportive confrontation most effectively.

Building Emotional Maturity, the Foundation for Living Happier Ever After

If your scores on the EMRF indicate that either you or your partner, or both of you, has some areas of immaturity, do not be discouraged. You can help each other gain greater maturity by using the simple method of supportive confrontation backed up by one-to-one time. This straightforward method of building emotional maturity is discussed at length in my book, written with Thomas P. Kelly, entitled *The Parent Book*. This book was written for parents who want to encourage emotional maturity in their children while, at the same time, building a lifelong relationship based upon mutual fondness, respect, and trust; however, *The Parent Book* is also an excellent guide to fostering the maturation process of people of any age and background.

The quality of the time together is what counts,

re than the quantity. One-to-one time is the in personal attention. To your lover, having oted and undivided attention is worth hours of comp ng for your recognition with the children, the office, or all the other distractions in a busy household. Your partner needs exclusive time with you and will benefit from the powerful message it conveys: "I care about you."

Let's start with "support."

One-to-One Time

Try as best you can to set aside twenty minutes of one-to-one time every day. It won't always be easy but, even if you do it only four or five times a week, it will have a positive effect on your relationship. Actually, the activity is less important than the fact that you are giving your full and serious attention to your partner.

A word of caution. You may be tempted to use this time to confront your lover about some problem. If you yield to this temptation, you will put your partner in a difficult bind. He or she will want very much to spend the time with you, but also will want to avoid the confrontation and unpleasantness that go with it. Instead, keep this time with your lover free of criticism and controversy. Let it be a time for you and your partner to be together here and now, sharing your experiences and concerns, your needs and hopes. It is a time to show that you're genuinely interested in your partner's concerns in an intimate and private way.

Do not confuse one-to-one time with simple togetherness. Two people separately doing the same thing, such as going to a movie, are practicing togetherness. But that kind of togetherness does not, cannot, give the deeply implied messages, "I care about you." "I am available to you with all my attention." "Nothing is more important to me than you and your concern." "My interest in you is warm, positive, personal." *Just listen completely and nondefensively to all your partner's bragging and complaining.* (For a further discussion of one-to-one time, see p. 236.)

The Philosophy of Confrontation with Support

Confrontation is a general term for challenge, criticism, or any kind of complaint that produces some negative feelings. Loving support provides the safety of unconditional acceptance. The combination of confrontation with support has been found to be the most civilized way of dealing with conflicts.

By using this approach, you and your partner will help each other's maturation and build a better relationship. A person who receives only support will remain weak and spoiled, self-centered and incompetent. A person who receives only challenge, and possesses an active temperament, will inevitably become rebellious and resentful. A person who receives only challenge, and possesses a passive temperament, will inevitably become crushed. Supportive confrontation must not be confused with one-to-one time; in one-to-one time, by just really listening you will never be anything but totally supportive.

When confrontation accompanied by support is used consistently, your partner will not be prone to see you as an enemy, but will experience you as a close friend and supporter. The feelings you and your lover experience together during these encounters determine the kind and quality of relationship you build. Their force is irresistible. If the feelings are good, the relationship will satisfy you both. If bad, both you and your partner are in for a stormy ride.

Your style of relating is crucial. It determines the feeling quality of the relationship—how you feel about each other. If your involvement is personal and warm, if you respect your partner's individual viewpoint, the feeling will be good and your relationship will grow. But a relationship characterized by detachment, coldness, or arbitrary authority will frustrate and alienate your lover. Most love relationships fall into the broad middle ground between these extremes; that is to say, they are neither as bad nor as good as they might be. If you treat each other positively, showing that you care and support each other's efforts to become responsible and mature, each partner will be highly motivated to try to meet the other's needs and expectations.

The Emotional Maturity Rating Form can be used as an effective measuring tool to monitor your progress. Each month rerate each other to serve as a reminder if either of you slips in practicing new and better habits. In this way, your relationship will evolve into an equal partnership in which each of you looks after the other. This is what the ultimate love relationship is all about.

Here are some examples of how you can give confrontation with support:

1. "I know your tennis game was important to you. I want you to have your exercise and recreation, but it would be nice if you would show me how much you care about me by coming home on time."

2. "I ran three errands for you, and even though I know you appreciate it, it would be nice to hear you say 'thanks.'"

3. "I know how important it is for you to look your very best at work, but it would take a lot of pressure off of me if you would get up fifteen minutes earlier in the morning, so we don't have to rush to catch our train."

4. "I know that you love me very much, but you could really make your point if you would fill the gas tank up next time you use my car on Sunday evening."

5. "I'm glad you like our lovemaking, but you could help me enjoy it more if you'd let me know earlier in the day what's on your mind instead of surprising me five minutes before we go to bed."

I'm in a relationship that needs improving. Will it get better by itself if we are both patient?

First you have to define the area in which you need help—romantic attraction or emotional maturity. Immaturity problems seldom get better on their own. On rare occasions, an immature person will fall so in love with someone that he or she becomes highly motivated to work at emotional maturation.

The much more common pattern is that by banging their heads together, a couple gradually learns that certain things don't work. Through trial and error, they discover all the things that don't work and slowly, very slowly, they acquire a maturity of sorts.

Now that you have learned about the technique of supportive confrontation, you know how to help each other to learn patterns of mature behavior. Mature behavior is caring behavior, and caring behavior is the firm foundation for a lasting, fulfilling love relationship.

Sixty-three Ways to Build Maturity

Awareness

The EMRF gives you a tool for evaluating your partner's awareness: insight into feelings; motivation; availability and responsiveness to good or bad feelings; methods of coping with or avoiding various kinds of feelings; and adaptability of thinking patterns. Being an aware person increases your chances of making a successful adjustment to life, of dealing in constructive ways with your love partner, as well as with other people, helping you to bring out the best in yourself and in other people. What follows is intended to give you a better understanding of the various facets of awareness and how you can either get into, or stay out of, trouble.

Behavioral Traits of Emotional Maturity

Awareness	Relating
A-1 Knowing your own feelings	R-1 Caring about others
A-2 Knowing the feelings of others	R-2 Getting attention constructively
A-3 Being spontaneously expressive	R-3 Earning acceptance
A-4 Ability to discuss personal feelings	R-4 Earning approval from others
A-5 Coping with mixed feelings	R-5 Giving affectionate regard
A-6 Curiosity	R-6 Being socially responsible
A-7 Getting desires met constructively	R-7 Being considerate
A-8 Coping with fear	R-8 Making friends
A-9 Coping with anger	R-9 Coping with peer pressure
A-10 Accepting responsibility for failure	R-10 Expressing dissatisfaction constructively
A-11 Coping with frustration and disappointment	R-11 Reciprocating good treatment
A-12 Accepting and approving of self	R-12 Sharing in decision making
A-13 Coping with uncertainty	R-13 Keeping promises
A-14 Sorting out real and make-believe	R-14 Resolving conflicts constructively
A-15 Using imagination constructively	R-15 Willingness to share
	R-16 Becoming more likable
	R-17 Coping with mixed feelings toward people
	R-18 Responding well to opposite sex

Competence	Integrity
C-1 Applying energy and effort	I-1 Showing self-control
C-2 Using knowledge and skills	I-2 Waiting willingly
	I-3 Being truthful in statements

C-3	Being planful	I-4	Coping with unpleasant-ness
C-4	Showing initiative		
C-5	Showing creativity	I-5	Being persevering
C-6	Behaving with realistic expectations	I-6	Being fair
		I-7	Being neat
C-7	Showing self-reliance	I-8	Being reliable
C-8	Willingly takes on challenge	I-9	Being genuine in behavior
C-9	Showing appropriate caution	I-10	Accepting blame when at fault
C-10	Showing self-confidence	I-11	Respecting property rights of others
C-11	Being responsible		
C-12	Being motivated to succeed	I-12	Willingly shares in the work
C-13	Being goal-directed		
C-14	Showing high standards		
C-15	Being cooperative		
C-16	Showing flexibility		
C-17	Developing personal interests		
C-18	Solving problems effectively		

A-1 *Knowing your own feelings*

Listen to your feelings. They will tell you how you are experiencing life. Tell your partner about your good feelings and your bad feelings. Your partner will get to know you much better. There will be much less wrong guessing, less misunderstanding, less arguing, and much more empathy between you. Describe the frustration of having your great aunt's sterling sugar spoon "chewed up" by the garbage disposal. Share that breath-catching moment when, stumbling outside to get the morning paper, you saw a dew-bedecked spiderweb.

A-2 *Knowing the feelings of others*

Listen, really listen, to your partner, but listen not only to the words, listen to the feelings. Try to determine if the feelings behind the words are mostly good feelings or bad feelings. Is your partner bragging or complaining? You will know your partner better, communication will improve. Try not to be judgmental. Remember that a certain amount of bragging is healthy and that any complaint that is shared will be easier to take, will ease the pain.

A-3 Being spontaneously expressive

If our parents always made it safe for us to let our feelings be known, spontaneity would never be a problem. All children, when little, are spontaneously expressive. But exuberant and screaming little children impose an emotional burden on parents, so we are "trained," socialized, taught to be much more constrained. Later we may be asked, "How do you feel?" but by that time we have been fitted with our emotional straitjackets. Instead of being spontaneous, we say "Fine," which means "How should I know? I've been under wraps for so long." To help your partner become more spontaneous, give him or her a safe atmosphere.

A-4 Ability to discuss personal feelings

If our parents had not made us feel that anger was bad, that fear is shameful, that inadequacy and failure were unacceptable, then we would have been able to tell all. When we tell all, we build and cross the bridge of closeness. Closeness is what we all need to feel in order to be less alone. (This is everyone's core problem.)

Make it safe for each of you to share your intimate thoughts, your intimate feelings. Go into these deeper waters gradually, mutually. It will build trust, understanding, and the intimacy that you need.

Be discreet. There are a few things, very few, that your lover doesn't need or want to hear. So don't undo it all under the misguided notion that honesty is the ultimate virtue. Your caring love is the ultimate virtue. People who are brutally honest are just that, brutal.

Have your partner show you his or her safest place in the house and say, "Here, I will always listen without interruption until you are finished. Here you will al-

ways be safe with me. I promise never to use anything
you say against you. I am willing to know the real you."

A-5 Coping with mixed feelings

Almost everything in life has its good and bad sides.
For every pleasure there seems to be a price. It is said
that it is an ill wind indeed that blows no good at all.
We learn from the pain of our mistakes. We both love
and hate to get up in the morning, to go to work, to
solve our daily problems.

If your lover is unhappy with you, it's not the end of
the world. Accept the inevitability of both appreciating
and resenting your lover.

Try to develop a good attitude about the painful
prices we pay for the benefits of our mutually rewarding
relationships. Remember that if the ecstasy is not worth
the agony, then perhaps it's time for a new love with a
better reward/pain ratio. Don't settle for too little, but
don't ignore or fail to appreciate what you do for each
other.

A-6 Curiosity

Those of us who are not interested in our surroundings
are not only less interesting but we are also less alive.
Explore each other's thoughts, feelings, and activities.
Get to really know each other. Then explore the world
together and compare your reactions. For those of us
who are really alive, each new door tends to open up
two new doors to more interesting experiences. So read
the libretto before you go to the opera. Read the art
books before you go to the museum. Open the doors to
a richer life for both of you.

A-7 Getting desires met constructively

Our desires can be the expression of a need, a want, or
sometimes of a deprivation complex. A need is something essential to our well-being. A want could enrich
our existence. Fulfilling a deprivation complex could be
a long-term project. We marry in order to be better
able to meet each other's needs.

One of our needs is to fulfill the unmet needs of our childhood. If we were refused an ice-cream cone, then we might like a sundae or two now, anytime, just to make up for those childhood losses. So expect to learn, and be willing to help your partner make up for some lost ground of fulfillment. In a way, you can be a second chance to be that parent that never could be. But if it gets extreme, you'd be wise to enlist the help of an experienced therapist. Pouring water into a sieve won't fill it. You will get better results if the holes are sealed. Something that is given and is not recognized and appreciated is something that is wasted, and that can seriously undermine any relationship.

You and your lover should discuss what you need from each other, and the ways that you can be sure that these needs will be met constructively, so that your mutual efforts will be recognized and appreciated and have no harmful side effects.

A-8 Coping with fear

Fear is a normal emotion. Its function is to protect. Crossing the street without caution could mean the end for any of us. When a fear is extreme and irrational, then instead of being protected, we are crippled. If your lover has a mild fear, you should be supportive and encouraging. If your lover has *a severe and irrational fear* (phobia) (and almost everyone has one or two), either try to be accepting, if it is a minor one, or encourage professional help if it is interfering unreasonably with his or her daily life. Remember that for the vast majority of us it is never too late to grow up.

A-9 Coping with anger

Anger, like fear, is normal. It typically results from frustration, and we all know life is really full of that. It is not whether we experience anger or not that is the key to a good adjustment, it is whether our resentment is expressed in a constructive way. If we always told everybody off, we would probably end up with nobody. It is constructive to deal with those frustrations that we truly can do something about. Usually this will require a certain amount of tact.

In dealing with your lover, it is wise to talk about how you frustrate each other. Then solve the problem together. One of you is bound to have a better idea than the other. Respect each other's counsel. Experiment; find a better way to deal with repeated frustrations.

Fighting usually does more harm than good. Healthy discussion is a mature alternative. Listen uncritically to everything your lover has to say. Don't get defensive. The better you listen, the more you will understand. Then there will be more empathy, less alienation, better compromise.

A-10 Accepting responsibility for failure

It is true that nobody's perfect. When you fail at something, it is wiser and more mature to admit your limitations than to try to find a scapegoat. Your lover will appreciate and respect you more if you show a reasonable degree of humility, objectivity, and honesty. Try saying "I was wrong" in five different ways—the fifth will hurt a lot less than the first!

A-11 Coping with frustration and discouragement

Frustrations and disappointments are inescapable features of life. While they cannot always be avoided, we can certainly adopt a more realistic attitude toward them. My office walls display a copy of Murphy's Law— "Anything that can go wrong, will"—and a chart of the solar system, just to help me keep things in perspective. Robert Burns recognized that most of our plans go awry. That's no reason not to try again.

You and your lover can help each other build a more mature attitude by reminding each other that while many things may not work out, they are still worth the effort, for without trying nothing will work out. Help each other to become more realistic.

A-12 Accepting and approving of self

If you don't believe that you are okay (not perfect, but

okay and trying harder), then when your lover shows you acceptance and approval, you will be unable to believe it. It just doesn't fit your picture of yourself. It's like someone giving us a prize or reward for something we believe we didn't do; we believe there has been some mistake. But sometimes the mistake is on our part. We could all do with a little more belief in ourselves, for none of us is as incompetent or as unworthy as we tend to think. We are all trying and we all have some kind of a track record, but we have to believe in ourselves before our lovers' appreciation and praise can have a meaningful impact. Remind each other of your achievements.

A-13 Coping with uncertainty
We all make predictions about tomorrow, but none of us can do it with total certainty. Life is unpredictable in some ways, perhaps too many. If you share your worries *without dwelling on them,* you will be giving each other an important lesson about life and human nature—that we all worry. To a certain extent, worry sharpens us and prepares us better for dealing with the unexpected.

A-14 Sorting out real and make-believe
What is real is here and now, testable and provable. It is convincing. Make-believe is another dimension, theoretically possible but definitely unprovable. Wisdom is the ability to tell the difference, and to live by it.

You can help your lover become more realistic by providing more information when it is asked for. You can make it easier for your lover to inform you by asking for help rather than by getting defensive. When you listen to each other's ideas, raise questions tactfully. When statements of plans sound unrealistic, you can say, "I hear you, but I have a lot of questions about that." When you seem to run into a stalemate or dead end, suggest that you use other people as a sounding board and see if they can find any holes in what you believe may be unrealistic. You don't need to assume the entire burden for interpreting reality.

A-15 Using imagination constructively

Fantasy has many useful functions. It can and should be the rehearsal before taking action. Speculation anticipates possible things that can go wrong.

Fantasy, in the science-fiction vein, can be just plain fun. You can build a better relationship with your partner by sharing your fantasies, even your way-out fantasies, those that we all have but have been taught to hide. To the extent that we hide our fantasies, we prevent our lovers from knowing us more fully, and thus limit the amount of acceptance we can have. But don't go overboard and tell all your fantasies at once. Getting to know each other should be a gradual process, not one that panics.

As you get to know each other better you will grow close, your critical comments will become more acceptable, and you can have a great deal of fun by building a life based on shared fantasies, some of which might come true, others which you might only share the pleasure of pursuing together.

Relating

The following will give you a deeper insight into the issues of relating, showing you how to encourage more mature relating in each other and how, at the same time, to build a stronger, more rewarding relationship.

R-1 Caring about others

A mature person is just as interested in the well-being of his lover as he is in his own well-being. This caring interest can be best shown by taking the initiative in showing a solicitous interest. Ask your partner, "How are you feeling? Is there anything I can do for you today?" Then follow through.

R-2 Getting attention constructively

Attention is soul food. We need it to reassure us that our lovers are still interested in us. Take some special notice of the existence of your partner. When you want

ʼntion, ask for it directly. When listening to your ʼrtner, *give your full and serious attention!* Be willing to turn off the TV or put down your newspaper.

R-3 Earning acceptance

Acceptance comes in two kinds. The first is tolerance, permitting your lover to be the person he or she is, despite the differences of opinion and imperfections. The second kind of acceptance is including your partner in your world. Let your partner know what's happening with you. Invite your partner to come along. As you show acceptance, it will be conducive to getting more acceptance from your lover. If your lover fails to notice your acceptance, point out how he or she is either missing it or not appreciating it.

R-4 Earning approval from others

We all need to be told that we are okay, doing well, to get those strokes of praise. It tells us that we are appreciated, valued, worthy—that we make a difference— and in a positive way. Any ego building that we give or receive won't cause an unduly swollen head if it is deserved, because it has been earned. Look after your lover's needs.

But be sure that your lover is also looking after your needs. If meeting each other's needs is not mutual, then you should point it out. Ask why. Find out what's wrong and do something about it.

R-5 Giving affectionate regard

If your lover is not very special to you, then perhaps you don't belong together. If you love your lover, say so. Your partner is not a mind reader. Be sure that you are giving some affection every day. It can be a special caress, a card, some flowers, a gift, remembering a birthday or anniversary, giving a small party, or any kind of a surprise that carries the message, "You are special to me, and I want you to know it."

R-6 Being socially responsible

As lovers, we are very sensitive to each other. People who are close can hurt each other most easily. Instead of being critical, you should always try to be ego-supportive.

But if you are asked for your honest opinion, you should give it. False praise will be recognized for what it is. And be polite with your lover. Good manners are not meant to be used only with strangers.

R-7 Being considerate

The considerate person thinks about the other person's needs before the event, not after. Before approaching, try to think about your lover's possible emotional state. You don't have to do any guessing. Ask, "What kind of a mood are you in?" or "What's on your mind?"

Before you get into a discussion, try to find out if this is a good time or if there is a better time. Try putting yourself in your partner's shoes. That will build empathy and a stronger relationship.

R-8 Making friends

When the chips are down, your lover is your best friend. If this is not so, then perhaps you are not with the right lover for you. A friend is someone who accepts you unconditionally, problems and all. Friends help each other and look after each other's best interests. Friends give, but they also feel comfortable in asking. Ask yourself if you like, respect, and trust your lover. If all the answers are not yes, then there is a problem that the two of you should be working on. Find out what it is, then agree to work on it together.

R-9 Coping with peer pressure

If you are yielding to negative pressure from your friends or lover, then you are trying to buy love, and you can't buy love. You may be able to buy pretense for a while, but not true romantic interest or mature, caring love.

Stand up for yourself. It's not too bold to ask your friends or lover if they want a slave or a yes man. Tell your lover you want to be partners. Really mature people do not want someone they can control. They want a partner who has conviction, who can insist upon getting respectful treatment, as well as giving affection and interesting companionship.

R-10 Expressing dissatisfaction constructively

If you have a complaint and don't tell your partner about it right in the open, then the price will be paid sooner or later, usually in the form of some kind of passive-aggressive sabotage. There will be something that is forgotten or misplaced. There is likely to be some kind of tit for tat.

In order to deal with dissatisfaction in a more mature way, we need to confront, but this confrontation can and should be done in a supportive way. You can say, "I know you care about me, but there is something we need to talk about, and I hope you won't feel that I'm attacking you."

R-11 Reciprocating good treatment

Looking after each other's well-being is what a good relationship is all about. If you are doing all the giving and not getting very much, then a tactful, supportive discussion is called for. It is not indecent to remind your partner that lately the giving has been pretty much a one-way street. Ask what happened to the fairness doctrine in your home.

R-12 Sharing in decision making

If one or both of you are making moderate-size or major decisions on your own, then you have only a partial and not a very full relationship. One of my patients called that being married-single, legally married but still operating in a unilateral way, as though there were no relationship. When decisions are made together, there is mutual investment in the relationship and your relationship will grow stronger.

When decisions are made separately, you are either withholding involvement or actively moving in the direction of an emotional divorce. Remember that most legal divorces began years earlier in a series of steps toward emotional divorce. Often, by the time the divorce papers are signed, one of the partners has almost completed the emotional divorce. So be on the lookout for unilateral decisions. They mean that there is dilution or a lack of commitment to the relationship. Marriage means together.

R-13 Keeping promises
Promises represent trust and caring. Don't make any promise that you do not really intend to keep. It is better to make fewer promises and keep them all than to set up your partner for disappointment. Unkept promises are remembered long after many of those promises that were kept have been forgotten.

None of us likes disappointment. When your lover fails to keep a promise, don't try to ignore it or excuse it. A tactful confrontation will usually lead to greater maturity and a stronger relationship. Hidden resentments don't build a strong relationship.

R-14 Resolving conflicts constructively
Disagreements are unavoidable. No two people could possibly agree on everything. So expect disagreements, but don't believe that disagreements have to result in a fight. In the typical fight, one partner is trying to overwhelm or overpower the other with the superiority of his or her knowledge, judgment, or wisdom. The only time you "win" a fight is when the fight benefits both partners. You should never want to overpower, defeat, antagonize, or alienate your best friend and staunchest supporter.

If you are so selfish or insecure that you have to have everything your way, then you are not mature enough for a really good relationship. Fighting should be reserved for your real enemies. Your partner should be your best friend, and you don't need to defeat or antagonize your best friend. When you harm your friend you weaken that person's desire to look after your best interests. Mature people search earnestly for a reasonable compromise, each being willing to give ground for the other person's benefit.

R-15 Willingness to share

If you find that you are competing with your partner, then you have an unresolved ego problem. You are doubting your adequacy. If you are trying to prove your adequacy by outdoing your partner, you may pick up a few temporary ego points, but the price you are paying is too high. You are causing animosity and insecurity in your best friend. Your ego problem can be resolved in a much healthier fashion through professional guidance. That way you develop a sense of adequacy that is honestly earned and deserved, and keep your lover happy at the same time. Lovers who are competitors are children in adult bodies.

R-16 Becoming more likable

Mature lovers are ready, willing, and able to both give and receive constructive criticism. In this way we can help each other to gain better respect and approval from each other and from other people as well. Try to make a pact with your lover to give each other honest and helpful criticism about how each of you can become more likable. Take the advice in a good-natured and appreciative spirit, and then put it to work for yourself and for the relationship.

R-17 Coping with mixed feelings toward people

In any relationship, there are going to be both feelings of appreciation and resentment. And it is much more intense in both ways with a lover. It is true that we always hurt the one we love, but we can certainly develop a reasonable attitude and try to understand that a certain amount of pain and disappointment will be inevitable. One misunderstanding doesn't mean that your lover has stopped loving you, or that the world has come to an end. Mature people accept that there will be some hurt, but work hard to keep it at a minimum.

R-18 Responding well to the opposite sex

If you don't like the opposite sex, you are carrying forward a very serious problem from your childhood, and you are definitely not mature enough to have a serious relationship. For those who dislike the opposite sex, counseling should come before marriage. It is just as important to like, trust, and respect your partner as it is to experience romantic excitement.

Competence

In order to gain the full benefit of being effective persons, it is also essential to believe in ourselves, to understand that our achievements have not resulted from luck or circumstance but from our own efforts. As we believe in ourselves and this respect for our accomplishments is recognized, appreciated, and reinforced by the expressed admiration of our loving partners, then we will experience the self-confidence that completes the satisfaction of being competent persons. The following shows ways for lovers to stimulate and encourage the continuing development of competence.

C-1 Applying energy and effort

Only using our energy in constructive ways will bring results. Yet we all wish for the easy way, and would prefer to be taken care of by our partner. Ask your partner what needs to be done, and do it. In addition to offering your help, do some of the work together, and you'll find that it can often be more fun. Be willing to do the job your partner's preferred way sometimes, even if you like your way better. Applying your energies in these ways will build maturity and improve your relationship at the same time.

C-2 Using knowledge and skills

Learning is a lifelong challenge. The mature person

wants to know more, to develop more skills and abilities. Your attitude is crucial. If you are willing to learn and make the necessary efforts you will. When you share your knowledge and skills with your partner you will be helping each other to become more effective people. Never make your partner feel like a dummy. Your challenge is to strengthen your partner, not to undermine self-confidence.

C-3 Being planful

Some people believe that planning destroys the chance for spontaneous pleasure. But, by thinking ahead, you will increase the chances that things can and will work out as you would like. Very few good dinners happen without at least a little planning. Do a little planning with your lover about assuring that you will have some time alone together. Then when you are alone there will be increased chances that nature can take its course and you will have the opportunity for lovemaking or a picnic or watching the sunset together.

C-4 Showing initiative

One of the most common problems seen by therapists is some symptomatic result of passivity. It is usually depression. Doing nothing will usually get you nothing. Both you and your partner should make sure that both of you are taking the initiative to suggest new things to do and better ways to do routine things. If your lover is unduly passive, it's time for some gentle but persistent confrontation. Let your lover know that both of you are suffering from a constricted existence. Encourage your lover to take the responsibility to help get things started, and be sure to reward all such efforts.

C-5 Showing creativity

Every one of us has tremendous creative potential. If you think for a minute about your dreams, you will realize that inside your brain there exists a very accomplished playwright, sometimes called your dream writer. Many dreams that are completed by this dream writer, who is a very real part of your inner potential, have original, organized characteristics. Your writer can do what a successful playwright does: develop characters, establish a setting, design props, write a script, and finally produce an ending. Even though most of us are not Arthur Millers or William Saroyans, we do have a lot more creative potential than we realize.

Dreaming is only one area for possible creativity. You and your partner should encourage each other to express your creative urges, but be careful about critical comments. When you tell your partner that he or she is off base, be sure that you are tactful enough to support his or her ego. The message should be, "Your idea is weird, but you are okay. Some of your other creative ideas were much better."

C-6 Behaving with realistic expectations

Mature, competent people have a great deal of respect for reality. While they may have great expectations, they know Murphy's Law, that anything that can go wrong will go wrong, if not this time, then next time—if not sooner, then later. Murphy, whoever he really was, reminds us that things will take longer and cost more than expected and that things will go wrong at the worst possible time.

Try to be accepting of your lover's great expectations, but gently, tactfully remind your partner of things that may have been overlooked. Don't puncture the balloon. Your attitude is critical. It should be one of helpful, supportive reminding, not one of criticism.

C-7 Showing self-reliance

If you are not resourceful, you should be practicing to become so. You will be more grown-up in the true sense of the word when you have learned how, and are willing, to go shopping, make a meal, use a household gadget, or fix minor things on your car, if these are things you have never done before. As you become a more self-sufficient adult you will feel less helpless, have more personal respect, and you will win appreciation and admiration from your partner. Your partner will have a stronger mate and you will both have a better relationship. So encourage your partner to become a more self-sufficient person. Be sure to praise your partner's efforts, and ask your partner to praise yours.

C-8 Willingly taking on challenge
Self-doubt plagues us all, though to different degrees. But if we don't take on a challenge, we most assuredly will not be able to master it. Try to understand your lover's reluctance to try something new because failure may result. While being supportive, encourage your lover to try. Mutual support will show your love and it will build a strong relationship.

C-9 Showing appropriate caution
When you drive carelessly, dangerously, you are being unwise and unkind to yourself, to the other drivers, and to your lover. You may think your lover is "safe" at home. Your lover is not safe. He or she has a considerable emotional investment in your life, your health, your well-being. By showing reasonable caution, you are looking after yourself and your lover in a more mature fashion. If your lover takes unnecessary chances, it's probably time for some supportive confrontation.

C-10 Showing self-confidence
Self-confidence means that we genuinely believe in ourselves. It means that in taking on a new challenge, we are not merely hoping to succeed, but that we believe we have a good shot at it, a good chance of succeeding. Self-confidence does grow by building a good track record, but it grows fastest and deepest when it is recognized and favorably commented upon by someone who is very important to you, like your lover. You each have the ability to help improve each other's self-confidence. So give all the reinforcement that is deserved.

C-11 *Being responsible*

Responsible people take care of their obligations without needing to be reminded. As you and your partner meet your commitments to each other, you can eliminate the cause of nagging. You will be growing up more, looking after each other better, and building a stronger relationship. When your lover fails to be responsible, ask if that is how love is shown. It's okay to remind your lover that actions speak louder than words. You can avoid an argument by being supportive in your confrontation. A little embarrassment won't hurt, and should produce better results.

C-12 *Being motivated to succeed*

If you don't have enough ambition to achieve some level of success in life, then someone is going to have to look after you, and it will be on his or her terms, whether it's your lover or the public welfare department. If your lover supplies all the ambition in your relationship, then you are in reality a private welfare case, and that will not give you much status.

No person can feel really grown-up unless he or she can develop some skills that will be recognized in the job marketplace or that can serve as a needed and respected support of the partner who is gainfully employed. If your lover is trying to escape from growing up by hiding in your arms, it is probably time for some loving, gentle, persistent confrontation.

C-13 *Being goal-directed*

Aimlessness is the enemy of success. If your partner does not have some fairly specific goal, encourage a discussion of what may be behind it. You can suggest to your partner that taking an interest test may be helpful in finding and pursuing a meaningful vocational goal. If your partner lacks social or recreational goals, or is not looking after his or her health, you should look for a possible underlying depression or lack of self-confidence. Confrontation and encouraging professional help is not nagging. If you care enough, you will motivate your lover to pursue life in a more effective way.

C-14 Showing high standards

Sloppy people usually look after their lover partners in sloppy ways. The sloppy adult is really a little child who wishes for success the easy way. You should tell a partner with such a deluded expectation that there is no free lunch. Only doing the job right will bring success. If your confrontation is given in a supportive way—a way that challenges the development of better products and greater self-respect—you will be genuinely helping your partner to grow up and you will be appreciated for your help.

C-15 Being cooperative

Two people can lift a log that one person cannot budge. In a good relationship both partners should have a mature attitude about combining their talents or abilities to work together to achieve common goals. It's a wise idea to discuss your respective talents and how you can work on projects together. You should take turns at being the leader, and be willing to use your partner's approach at times.

If your partner is not very good at cooperation, you should mention that marriage means together, and if he or she can't or won't join forces, then ask what the purpose of the relationship is. If this kind of inquiry looks like it may be starting a war, ask your lover why he or she is not trying to be more supportive. Only a very resistive partner—one who is not truly a partner—will fail to respond to this kind of appeal.

C-16 Showing flexibility

After doing therapy for forty years, Lawrence Kubie concluded that the major difference between a neurotic person and a normal one is that the neurotic person is rigid, while the normal person is flexible. Of course, it's a matter of degree. Flexibility is the readiness, willingness, and ability to consider new information and to appropriately adjust our course of action to achieve an originally sensible goal. The less fearful, the less ego-defensive, and the more imaginative we are, then the more flexible we can be. Being flexible in the way we approach issues with our lover also shows our respect for his or her needs and wishes. If your partner is not being flexible, explore with him or her what might be causing the rigidity.

C-17 Developing personal interests

A person with a passion is more alive and is usually a much more interesting and exciting companion. People who have not developed some strong vocational or recreational interest are usually suffering from insufficient stimulation by an interested friend. If your partner has not developed strong personal interests, then you can and should be that friend. Offer a richer variety of experiences, and encourage your partner to get involved. Say, "Try it, you'll like it!"

C-18 Solving problems effectively

This is where all the seventeen other traits of the competent person come together. You and your partner should keep in mind the steps in problem solving: Define the problem and the goal, collect the needed information, develop and carry out your plan, expect that you may need to modify your plan, never stop trying, work on it together—that is necessary. Listen to each other's ideas. Use the good ones, but don't put your partner down for offering to be helpful.

Integrity

You and your partner can help each other to develop improved self-discipline and foster more ethical behavior by approaching each other about the appropriate issue using the following guidelines.

I-1 Showing self-control

In a child, impulse rules unreasonably over control. In

an adult, control rules reasonably over impulse. Self-control is a matter of personal pride, of self-respect. When we overindulge in food or alcohol or some other drug, we tend to be married to our addiction, and therefore less married to our lovers. If this is true of your relationship, it's time for supportive confrontation.

I-2 *Waiting willingly*
The key to patience is having a realistic attitude. One restaurant has a sign that reads PLEASE BE PATIENT. IT TAKES TIME TO PREPARE GOOD FOOD PROPERLY. In other words, please be realistic. You and your lover can be kind to each other by gently reminding each other that while wishes might move at the speed of light, few of the daily events of life come anywhere near matching that speed.

I-3 *Being truthful in statements*
When we are not telling the truth, the whole truth, we are either being ego-defensive to avoid embarrassment or are trying to manipulate our partners. In the first instance, we hurt ourselves by cowardly escapism and the consequent loss of self-respect. By manipulating our partners, we hurt them and ourselves by cheating. We deprive our partners of the respectful treatment they deserve and we deprive ourselves of self-respect as well.

Honesty is the best policy. Almost always in marriage counseling, the partner who has been deprived of the truth says that he or she would rather know than to be kept in the dark or allowed to guess and to suffer from wild and negative imagining. Affairs or sexual indiscretions are a major exception to this rule. If your partner seems to be untruthful, then, for the sake of your relationship, you need to discuss how mistrust is undermining your partnership.

I-4 *Coping with unpleasantness*
Life is full of unpleasantness, but once we recognize

and accept the inevitability of a certain amount of unpleasantness, pain, and discomfort, we will find life to be more agreeable. The key here is to develop a realistic attitude toward life's unpleasantnesses as just a part of the price we must pay for the rewards we want. If indicated, help your partner to adopt a more realistic attitude and ask your partner to help you. Tell your partner when you have a headache; a loving touch is a better curative than silent stoicism.

Be willing to help your partner deal with the unpleasantness he or she faces. You will be helping to build character and a better relationship at the same time.

I-5 Being persevering

Procrastination will not get the job done; it will earn neither your own self-respect nor the admiration of your partner. Here, as with most traits of character, only grit and determination will conquer those childish tendencies to procrastinate or to assume someone else will do it for you. There is just no substitute for digging in. But there's no reason you can't encourage and help each other whenever possible.

I-6 Being fair

When you take unfair advantage of your lover, you are undermining your partner and the relationship at the same time. Those who live by a double standard should be reminded that deep within they cannot have a great deal of self-respect. Self-respect can only happen when we really live by the golden rule of treating others as we wish to be treated. In order to build a better relationship, you should question and challenge your partner when you are treated unfairly, as well as asking your partner to challenge you when you act unfairly.

I-7 Being neat

Littering the landscape of your home defiles your relationship and can be louder than words in saying that you don't have much self-respect or regard for your partner. Neatness and a reasonable degree of orderliness are ways that you can show that you care.

If you have a strong desire to be taken care of, you should be honest about that and pay for domestic help. If you want your lover to take care of you, then be sure that you are taking equally good care of him or her.

I-8 Being reliable

Marriage is a sacred commitment. When we marry, we repeat words that have profound meaning, but rare indeed is the person who reflects on the words that are said or what their deep implications are. In brief, we make the mutual commitment to look after each other in all major matters.

Immature lovers, no matter what their commitments are, wish to be taken care of, expect to be taken care of, and wind up aggravating the one they love by trying to guarantee they will be taken care of. The mature lover recognizes the commitments to look after the well-being of his or her partner and delivers on those commitments. Being unreliable will undermine your relationship. Unreliability should be gently but persistently confronted. Without such confrontation, your relationship will involve a child instead of a loving partner, no matter how much romantic excitement there is.

I-9 Being genuine in behavior

We were all genuine as children. We responded to sistuations in a natural and spontaneous way. We were sincere, at least up until a time when we developed the need for insincerity and had the mental ability to carry it out. Insincerity is an acquired trait, usually used to cope with a threatening environment, one filled with manipulations and countermanipulations. If your partner behaves in insincere ways, it's time to point out that your love relationship's environment is different, that your partner is dealing with a different significant-other person, one who is able and willing to give openness and acceptance, offering a relationship in which there is now safety to be one's self.

I-10 Accepting blame when at fault

A child has not yet had much of a chance to build up a strong sense of self-worth, so it is only natural for a child to avoid admission of wrong-doing. After all, the little self-worth that the child feels will be diminished by that admission. But as adults, we all have some kind of a track record; we know that we have a reasonable amount of worth. There is no good reason to carry this childish, defensive attitude forward into our relationship with someone for whom we have esteem and appreciate. It is more mature to own up to wrongdoing, accept the amount of embarrassment, and try to do better next time.

I-11 Respecting the property rights of others

Taking good care of the possessions of your lover is a way of showing respect and caring. It shows self-respect as well. When you use your lover's car, you can show your love by bringing it back washed and with a full tank of gas. If your possessions are not well looked after, once again it's confrontation time, for that's the principal way we help each other to grow up.

I-12 Willingly shares in the work

Sharing in the work shows your self-discipline and is part of the decent and respectful treatment you accord your partner. Adopting a positive attitude about chipping in with the work shows your partner that you appreciate what is done for you. Try surprising your partner by doing one of his or her customary chores. If you make it a habit, you will endear yourself to your lover and build a strong relationship. So wash your lover's car, do the laundry. It will make an adult out of you.

Chapter Six

♡ ♡ ♡

Love
in Trouble

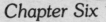

ONE IS MATURE

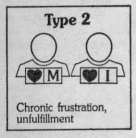

Type 2

♥ M   ♥ I

Chronic frustration,
unfulfillment

About one-third of the couples in my practice, and possibly everywhere, are Type Twos. They make up the second largest category of lovers with whom I work. (Type Fives are the largest.) Type-Two couples often come in for therapy because one inflicts suffering through his or her immature behavior. They are in love with each other, but one is frustrated or disappointed in the other as a result of that partner's immaturity causing misunderstandings. Yet if Type-Two couples separate or divorce, it is an unwise and unfortunate mistake!

The problem with Type-Two relationships is that one member of the couple has a serious problem with emotional maturity. Each person rates his or her mate with a high romantic attraction score, but only one of the two is reasonably mature. The immature person acts out his or her immaturity by either neglecting the partner or making unreasonable demands which first aggravate and can eventually destroy the relationship. He or she may pursue extramarital affairs, may spend too much time on the job, may not express true feelings. As a result, the couple may not know why, but they're aware something is wrong. They may even falsely assume they just weren't meant for each other.

Often they break up, especially if they're not already married. What they probably don't realize is that once the less-mature partner does some growing up, most of their problems can be solved. The couple can split up, stay together and suffer, or seek professional help and become a Type-One couple.

We're in a Type-Two situation, but I don't think you can ever find the perfect partner. What should we do?

You will never find everything you're looking for in one person; that's for sure. Part of being mature is understanding the importance of trade-offs and compromise. If you are indeed in a Type-Two relationship, you have the main requirement for a happy relationship: You are both romantically excited about each other. The problems in maturity can be resolved by making the necessary efforts. Go with your partner for help. If your partner won't agree to accompany you, then he or she is probably the one with the more serious maturity problem. Once your partner sees your determination to seek professional help on your own, sooner or later he or she will almost always go along with you.

Because your romantic attraction is mutually high, your partner has a strong interest in maintaining the relationship. Realizing he or she could lose you, your partner will be motivated to accompany you to seek professional guidance. Start counseling on your own and there's a very good chance your partner will join the program. If you meet resistance, you may have to bring up the possibility of separation—or even divorce. You may have to demonstrate the seriousness of your intentions by consulting an attorney and, if necessary, start proceedings. This is a last resort—but it usually gets attention.

Try to remember that although the divorce rate is high, people are often quite resistant to breaking up a marriage, especially one in which there is a high degree of romantic attraction. Your partner would probably prefer working out the problems to losing you outright. Instead of seeking the perfect mate, look to improve your existing relationship.

Type-Two Blues

It is relatively easy for Type-Twos to get an accurate diagnosis of their problem because it is so clear-cut. Both have strong romantic interest, but one of the partners in the relationship is not treating the other in a caring, considerate manner. Immaturity is causing the lover to jeopardize the relationship. However, the willingness to seek professional guidance and some hard work on the part of the immature partner, combined with a lover who is willing to help, will bring significant improvement in the relationship.

The immature member of the couple is having a problem in one or more of the four aspects of maturity. It could be an awareness problem.

When one isn't aware of one's own feelings, it's very difficult to communicate about them. The partner is forced to guess. And most guesses are wrong and can be destructive. For example, the immature partner may have rated his lover as 290 on the RAQ scale, but he didn't feel safe enough to reveal his strong feelings, resulting in his partner doubting his love for her.

Some of us are taught at an early age that we shouldn't show our feelings, that "big boys" and "big girls" don't cry. We can be suffering from childhood conditioning that makes it almost impossible for us to reveal our true feelings. When our lovers ask a question, we answer with a side step. "Are you hungry?" is answered with, "It's not time for dinner." "Yes" or "No" would have been the direct, appropriate response.

The person who is not aware cannot empathize with

another. It's hard to be sensitive to others when
denying the same emotions in yourself. You
respond appropriately if you don't know how.
sponse that the unaware person does make usually
makes the situation worse. He or she may gamble,
drink, stay late at the office, or have an affair. A void is
created in the relationship between the two partners
and eventual breakup is likely. People who cannot
express their feelings cannot expect a good relationship
until they learn to be more aware and to share their
personal feelings with others.

One of the problems with the immature partner in a
Type-Two relationship is that he or she may make
unreasonable demands on the other partner and the
relationship. This partner may expect to be taken care
of. A man may expect his wife to wait on him as if she
were his slave, to take care of him the way his mother
took care of him when he was a little child. If the
immature partner is a woman with this problem, she,
too, probably wants to be taken care of. She may think
that, in exchange for her body as a sexual object, a
man should do everything to take care of her other
needs.

Fear is one of the most common manifestations of the
immaturity problem seen in Type Twos. If one of the
partners is phobic about closeness, there isn't going to
be a very close relationship. The adult dealing with fear
suffers from what I call the moth-and-flame syndrome,
which is invariably rooted in childhood. The moth is
drawn by the brightness and warmth of the flame, but
when he gets too close, he gets burned. A person is
drawn to a warm and loving relationship, but having
been burned before—probably by his or her parents—
panics and runs as the fire gets hotter, usually at the
first sign of conflict or tension. (For a further discussion
of moth-and-flame syndrome, see p. 178.)

*I've been in three bad marriages. The Love Test
materials make me think I have a fear problem. Will I
ever be able to get close to someone?*

Yes. The capacity is alive in all of us, no matter how deeply buried it may be under a blanket of fear.

Your problem will be resolved most quickly with counseling and a partner who finds you romantically exciting and is also emotionally mature. It will certainly help if you find him desirable too.

While reassurance and security are the standard remedies for fear, I have often seen women who get so romantically excited about a man that, with that man, they experience orgasm for the first time in their lives. I'm not saying that romantic sex is, in itself, a cure for fear, but a great deal of desire can help overcome fear. Much research has been done on this subject and the evidence is clear: Strong desire can reduce fear.

Then there is the person who cannot show anger. He or she is forced to sabotage the love relationship by expressing anger in indirect ways. This person, without actual conscious intent, sabotages his or her partner through passive-aggressive behavior.

Jani is feeling angry at Rich, but instead of directly confronting him with her angry feelings—which frighten her—she swallows them. Later, she manages to forget the steak broiling in the oven until it has become thoroughly well done. Rich, of course, loves it rare. When the passive-aggressive partner continues these kinds of actions on a regular basis, the relationship may end. Then this partner, typically with a shrug of the shoulders, will say, "We just weren't meant for each other."

Being able to express one's anger honestly and appropriately is one aspect of maturity. The person who cannot express anger needs to learn the courage to confront. I'm not encouraging fighting; I am encouraging both partners to speak out what is on their minds *at the time* they are experiencing angry feelings—not two weeks later. Confrontation does not have to start a fight. Love partners can express their frustrations in ways that do not accuse their partners or put them down.

The inability to accept responsibility for failure is

another of the most common problems immature people have to face up to. Some people just can't say, "Hey, I goofed. I was wrong."

A person with so little self-esteem that he or she never can admit to being wrong is suffering from a severe inferiority complex and needs professional help. This person is terrified that if he is proven wrong on one fact, he will be revealed to the world as a total failure. The need to be right usually encompasses all areas of human behavior. The partner, denied the "right to be right," becomes angry, because it is very frustrating to live with someone who has to be correct all the time.

Then there are those who want everything to be perfect. They don't understand that flexibility is one of the key factors in maturity. I call these people Ceiling People. If one little detail isn't perfect, they go through the ceiling. They may become hysterical if the florist delivers pink roses instead of red. Ceiling People concentrate on the hole instead of the doughnut. To the Ceiling Person, the glass is always half-empty—never half-full. Floor People are the opposite of the Ceiling People; they are well-grounded in reality, satisfied to have the doughnut and not mind the hole in its center. They know there's nothing they can do about it. For Ceiling People, relationships are difficult because at the first sign of disappointment trouble arises.

Another problem I see often in Type Twos is what I call the China Doll complex. This is a holdover from the days of post-Victorian society, before the women's movement. The message from the China Doll is, "Don't touch me—you'll break me." The China Doll puts distance between herself and others. You don't upset the China Doll; you don't tamper with the status quo; you don't let the realities of the world infringe on the China Doll's fantasy life. If you do, it's disaster time, hysteria time, and time-out for the relationship. Effective counseling can help to resolve the China Doll complex.

Some people with insufficient self-esteem to stand on

their own think that the treatment they get from their partners is a one hundred percent reflection of themselves. If they don't approve of themselves deep down inside, they will never be able to believe that someone else approves of them. When you feel unworthy, you can't believe and accept worthy treatment from a partner. As a result, each disagreement, no matter how minor, can be interpreted as total rejection. These people can become obsessive and excessive in their need to be reassured that everything is going all right. Unable to handle any kind of uncertainty, they have a terrible need to know—now! They don't want to hear, "I'll call you later." They want to hear, "I'll call you at three-thirty." If the phone hasn't rung by three-thirty, they're sure they've done something wrong and have been found out.

These people are difficult companions for a walk through the woods of life because they are a constant drain. They drain energy instead of giving it.

The Type-Two immature partner can give his or her lover a hard time; just how hard depends on how immature he or she is, how readily he or she will work to effect change in himself or herself, and how willing he or she is to accept coaching from a lover and/or sessions with a counselor.

Our Love Just Died

Many Type-Two couples have the sadly mistaken belief that love dies and that their romance is over because, while things were great once, the spark is out; the ember is cold and love has died.

True Romantic Chemistry Never Dies

The great tragedy of a Type-Two divorce or separation is that these people don't understand that true romantic chemistry doesn't die. The chemistry may appear to fade or to wane; it could be hidden under a blanket of fear, anger, hurt, or disappointment. That is only because the immature partner has been so abusive that the mature partner became discouraged and gave up. When true romantic chemistry exists, as it does with all Type Twos, the "dead" love can be revived—because it isn't really dead. It is suffering from neglect; weakened by uncaring treatment. But it can be restored to full health.

If your relationship is a Type Two and you are living with the fallacy that your love has died, try using some or all of these tips. The romantic excitement you once shared will resurface.

Bessell's Fifty Ways to Keep Your Lover

1. Show your feelings and report them to your lover as accurately as possible.
2. Be sensitive to the feelings of your lover.
3. Be spontaneously expressive.
4. Discuss what you are thinking and feeling.
5. Try to cope with your ambivalence and discuss your mixed feelings.
6. Be curious: about yourself, your lover, and the world around you.
7. Try to cope with fears; don't hide from them.
8. Try to cope with anger; don't bury it or deny it.
9. Accept responsibility for failure. Nobody's perfect.
10. Ask for your partner's help to resolve your feelings of frustration when they occur.
11. Try to feel good about the good parts of yourself, despite your limitations.
12. Accept uncertainty; life and love are full of it.
13. Differentiate between fantasy and reality.
14. Show others that you care by your caring behavior.
15. Respect the value of others.
16. Develop a more helpful and positive attitude. It's the only thing that works.

17. Make and keep other friends in addition to your lover.
18. Do your share of the work.
19. Express dissatisfaction tactfully and constructively.
20. Reciprocate good treatment.
21. Share the decision making with your partner.
22. Keep your promises.
23. Resolve conflicts without fighting. Try to see your partner's point of view.
24. Share possessions.
25. Appreciate criticism as something helpful.
26. Be equally courteous to members of both sexes.
27. Show your enthusiasm.
28. Give your best effort to everything.
29. Become more organized.
30. Show your creativity.
31. Have realistic expectations of other people and of situations.
32. Show your self-reliance.
33. Take on challenges.
34. Show self-confidence.
35. Be responsible.
36. Set high standards and keep them.
37. Be cooperative.
38. Be flexible.
39. Develop hobbies and personal interests.
40. Demonstrate self-control.
41. Wait patiently when you must wait.
42. Don't lie.
43. Finish whatever you start.
44. Be fair.
45. Be reliable.
46. Accept blame when you are at fault.

47. Respect the property rights of others.
48. Be sincere.
49. Cope with the unpleasant in a pleasant manner.
50. Give your partner your full and serious attention *every day*!

Rx for Type-Two Relationships

The Type-Two couple has a problem with one partner's maturity, but because each partner has a strong romantic attraction for the other, the couple can be on the road to a Type-One relationship in a short period of time.

The partner with the low amount of maturity needs to grow up, and the already-mature partner can be very helpful.

Professional guidance will help the immature partner, and, together, the couple can practice improving their relationship. Even without therapy, the Type-Two couple who practices the winning ways can move toward becoming a Type-One couple.

- Never guess what your lover thinks or means. Ask, and you will avoid wrong or negative assumptions.
- Tactfully ask your lover if he or she would like your help to develop more mature behavior. Once you have permission, remind your partner of his or her commitment to practice more mature behavior. With your lover's permission, you can help raise his or her awareness of unproductive behavior patterns.
- Invest twenty minutes a day in one-to-one time (see p. 134).
- Ask yourself every day if you are treating your partner as though he or she has the same personality as some other important person in your past (a parent, perhaps). If you are, remind yourself of the differ-

ence between these two people, and strive to respond more appropriately to your partner.

- Don't get a divorce before seeking counseling.
- Help each other to grow up.

Chapter Seven

♡　♡　♡

Love in
Double Trouble

NEITHER IS MATURE

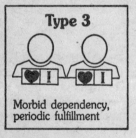

Type 3

Morbid dependency,
periodic fulfillment

Type-Three couples suffer from an unfortunate paradox: Both are very much in love, but both are very miserable. They enjoy intense moments of joy, but cope with a great deal of agony in between. Type Threes have one half the makings of a lasting relationship: They are very attracted to each other. Each person in the Type-Three couple gives the other a high score on the RAQ. But *each* person in the couple is limited by a lack of maturity.

But since maturity can be developed, and romantic attraction cannot be, Type Threes have the possibility of sharing the fulfilling and lasting love relationship they crave—*if* (or *when*) they get the help they need in growing up!

Since both partners in the Type-Three couple need to grow up, the possibilities for the future can be predicted. If neither person gets help, the couple will probably stay together for the rest of their lives, functioning poorly, moaning, complaining, fighting, and undermining each other, leaving their friends shaking their heads in wonder, "Why do they stay together?"

Or perhaps the more mature of the partners will get some professional help and will become more mature. When this happens, the couple will then have a Type-Two relationship. The newly matured person, because he or she matures and cares so much, can now help the other to grow up. If the second partner also matures, eventually the Type-Two relationship will become Type One.

It is possible, but unlikely, that the newly matured partner may say, "Hey, I know your game and it won't work. You're never going to grow up. I want out." Partners in a Type-Three relationship are reluctant to separate because of their strong mutual romantic interest. They are held together by the healthy, mutual romantic excitement that they share and, before growing up, by unhealthy, mutual morbid dependency.

Are there some people who are in love with each other but just shouldn't live together?

Yes, Type-Three people, who are romantically excited about each other but have severe immaturity problems. Although they have the capacity to give each other a great deal of pleasure in terms of companionship, sex, mutually exciting interests, and so on, they really shouldn't try marriage or living together until they improve their maturity.

They are not mature enough to give each other a happy marriage. Their immaturity will cause a great deal of pain, anguish, and anxiety. These people may get ten percent pleasure from each other, but the ninety percent pain they endure is just not worth the suffering.

There are other types of people who shouldn't have gotten together in the first place, as you can see on the Love Relationships Chart (p. 3)—Types Four, Five, Six,

Seven, Eight, and Nine. Naturally, Threes shouldn't be living together. For example, there are Few Type Fives who are happy living together. They have made two mistakes by getting married: there's not enough romantic attraction and one of the partners is too immature.

Couples who have Type-Six, -Eight, or -Nine relationships also have maturity problems. They are not mature enough to be married, and they don't make good roommates either. They haven't grown up and have a strong desire to be taken care of. They want a parent even more than a lover.

The Type-Three Dilemma

The typical problem with Type Threes is that in their mutual immaturity neither can assume responsibility for his or her shortcomings. On the conscious level, they think they are blameless; on the subconscious level, they think they are worthless. When something goes wrong, they are prone to blame the other person. They cannot see themselves at fault.

These people may see a counselor, but instead of admitting to their own problems, they end up in a standoff. They spend their session with the counselor blaming the other partner for the problems with the relationship. Each one wants and expects to be taken care of by the other partner.

The scenario is almost always the same: (1) the therapy isn't easy; (2) they get angry; (3) they blame the partner; and finally, (4) they meet one of the three fates of Type Threes.

The Three Fates

Because of its special nature, a couple with a Type-Three relationship will invariably end up in one of three ways:

They will eventually end in a bitter divorce.

They will get professional help and become Type Ones.

They will no nothing and continue to make each other miserable.

It is not unheard of for a Type-Three couple to divorce. In fact, if they do divorce, it is often in the early stages of their marriage. But some Type Threes, as in *Who's Afraid of Virginia Woolf?*, will battle frequently and have a trying love-hate relationship that could go on for years, surviving many breakups and makeups.

If a Type-Three couple separate, they usually expect that the next time they will find Mr. or Ms. Right, and everything will be "perfect." But the partners are making a false and unfortunate assumption, because Type Threes who divorce usually do so for the wrong reasons. They are not likely to find happier marriages with other people unless the next partners are much more mature and can help them grow up emotionally.

They also run the risk of remarrying a person who is more mature but with whom they don't have a strong mutual romantic attraction. The mature partner will treat the other well. Nevertheless, after a bitter Type-Three divorce, either or both partners may think like this:

"Gee, I've just come out of this terrible marriage, and miserable divorce."

"Gee, this person (my new lover) really loves me."

"This person treats me really well."

"My new partner likes my kids."

"I think I *should* marry this person."

But good treatment is not romantic love, and because the romantic excitement that existed with the first partner is not in the second marriage, the new marriage will not be fulfilling. The original lovers in the Type-

Three couple probably would have done better to stay together and work out their problems.

Type Threes rarely have civilized divorces. They often continue to carry on with unresolved resentments toward their old spouses. They part on bad terms and the bitterness can stay with them forever.

If they stay together, however, and do what's necessary to grow up, they can very significantly improve their relationship. Once there is growth and improvement in one of the lovers, and the other person notices it, the partner is encouraged. When one sees the partner making progress, hopes are built up so the other mate gets more involved in his or her own growing up. After the initial success period, maturation is slow going for Type Threes, but if the partners can stay with it and remember how good it felt when they first started to see changes, they can make it to a more mature level. But it does take perseverance.

Those Type Threes who choose to stay together and do not work at growing up will continue to have a series of ups and downs; they will fight and bicker, and often drink in an effort to escape, but they will be together until the bitter end.

Type-Three couples are capable of mutual pleasure, happy companionship, and great lovemaking. Type Threes are the kind of couple who can go away for a long weekend and have a wonderful time. At such times, they enjoy every moment together: They laugh; they tease; the sex is great; whatever problems they have seem minimal; and they are as joyful as two honeymooners. When they get home from the weekend, one of the partners notices that the newspapers are piled up in front of the door, a blatant statement to burglars that the house was left vacant over the weekend. "Why didn't you call the newspaper to stop delivery for the weekend?" The beauty of the weekend is forgotten and all that those magic moments together accomplished is buried in a mountain of curses, accusations, and tears.

Moth-and-Flame Syndrome

Type Threes always suffer from fear of a close relationship. Their severe vulnerability causes them to unconsciously create trouble. The trouble is a device used in an attempt to make them less vulnerable by creating safety through distance. Because it's unconscious, it lets them off the hook blame-wise. Because they can't trust their partners and each act of closeness intensifies their fears of being hurt, fearful partners have a strong need to create distance—especially after intimacy. So they play "safety" games as they practice intramarital warfare.

They are suffering from what I call the moth-and-flame syndrome. The moth is attracted to the light of the flame on a candle. It flies close, because to the moth the light means food. Attracted even closer, the moth gets burned and, henceforth, is afraid of fire. The moth may spend the rest of its life hovering near a flame, trying to get what it desires, but is unable to be satisfied for very long before fear sets in.

In their early years, people who are threatened by intimacy learn that closeness can be very painful. Usually, Mom or Dad, or both, failed to give the child adequate love and attention. Moving close to the parent in search of these things usually brought rejection and pain. When the child grows to be an adult, a high price is paid. The adult is fearful in close relationships.

However, as an adult, the emotionally damaged child can be cured and reclaimed for love. But he or she needs a loving, mature partner, and sometimes a good therapist. If teamed in a Type-Three relationship, the other partner has the same basic problem. Only a careful and steady diet of mutual, and steadily increasing, and justified provisional trust can improve this relationship and bring satisfaction to these partners.

Provisional Trust

Provisional trust works well between lovers who suffer from the moth-and-flame syndrome because it shows understanding and respect for the fearful place they are coming from. Each partner says to the other, "I understand that you don't trust me and I see your reasons in the light of what you experienced in close relationships in the past." But then each person offers some provisional trust, in very small amounts at first, to help the other see that improvement in their relationship really is possible.

Provisional trust is a one-time guarantee and serves as an experiment. "I'll trust you just this once on this one little thing," is all each partner commits to. Slowly, very slowly, the provisional trust is extended, from one situation to more, from one week to several weeks, and then to months. With positive efforts, the couple builds tiny milestones of trust; they build a new relationship based not on their past painful experiences but on their new positive experiences with closeness. In time they will build a mutually trusting relationship.

Type Threes Need Professional Guidance

It is very difficult to help Type Threes whose EMRF scores are low in two or more of the four maturity categories. They're frightened and distrustful and they behave much like children, expecting magical things to happen without much effort on their own parts. When nothing much happens in two or three sessions, they find one excuse or another to avoid counseling. They are sometimes too immature and afraid to hear what the counselor suggests to them.

Borderline Type-Three/Type-One couples, the ones

with a relatively high degree of emotional maturity, will stay with counseling and get good results. If the Type-Three partners are not too severely crippled but go for help, they will make significant improvement. Sessions for each person in the couple should be conducted privately, and then after some individual progress has been made, and there is sufficient trust in the therapist, the couple can attend sessions together.

There is hope for Type Threes! They have a chance of becoming Type Ones if they desire it enough, and work at it. Their lives can improve dramatically if they are willing and able to look at themselves and show persistent, strong, positive interest in each other.

The Borderline Type-Three/Type-One

Sarah and Dick were young professionals who were introduced by friends. Sarah was a branch manager for a cosmetic company; Dick was a lawyer. Both were immensely competent and their ambitions were well founded. Everyone who met them knew that Dick would become a partner in his law firm and that Sarah would end up as a vice-president in her company.

They both worked separately from each other (fourteen-hour workdays were not uncommon), but were very supportive of each other's ambitions and goals. Dick often helped brainstorm with Sarah and even thought up the name for a new hair coloring. Sarah listened to Dick practice his arguments before he gave them in court.

They were very happy together for long periods of time, and then suddenly war would break out. Sarah would complain that Dick didn't love her enough, wasn't attentive enough, worked too long, and wasn't interested in sex often enough. Dick rarely argued back; he would just shrug his shoulders and walk out of the door, disappearing for several hours. Sarah knew that Dick's mother had died mysteriously when he was a teen-ager, and since he refused to discuss it, Sarah

PERSONAL LOVE PROFILE

Number of Low Scores on   Romantic Attraction
Emotional Maturity Rating   Questionnaire (RAQ) Score
Form (EMRF)

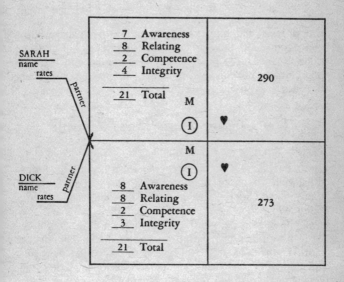

LOVE RELATIONSHIP TYPE_____ Borderline 3/1

Number of low EMRF Scores   *RAQ Scores*
0–20 low scores total   M   ♥ 220–300 strong attraction
21 or more low scores total   I   ♥ 200–220 borderline
                                   ♡ 180–200 weak attraction

Types of Love Relationships

Type 1 ♥ M ♥ M   Type 4 ♥ M ♡ M   Type 7 ♡ M ♡ M

Type 2 ♥ M ♥ I   [Type 5 ♥ M ♡ I]   Type 8 ♡ M ♡ I
                   [Type 5 ♡ M ♥ I]

Type 3 ♥ I ♥ I   Type 6 ♥ I ♡ I   Type 9 ♡ I ♡ I

was sure he was scarred emotionally and had a fear problem. Yet Dick was offended when Sarah suggested that he needed therapy, and Sarah would burst into tears when Dick countered by saying she needed the therapy. And Sarah couldn't stop her relentless demands on Dick.

Sarah and Dick could live together for years, with their not-unusual relationship. Or they could both get the professional guidance they need. Both are highly competent and have a good bit of integrity, but they need considerable help in their awareness and relating problems. There is every reason to believe they can become a Type-One couple.

The Classic Type-Three Couple

Mindy and Jeff met in school and married before they graduated. Each went directly from living at home during high school to living in a dorm at college, to their married life together in a small off-campus apartment. They were intelligent, well-educated, attractive, lazy, and immature. Before their marriage, neither had ever done his or her own laundry, made a bed, gone to the market, or cooked a full meal. Both were insecure, disorganized, and lacking in self-confidence. They had very similar problems and neither could keep his affairs straight—term papers were not turned in on time, car keys were lost, books were rarely returned to the library.

Once or twice a month, Mindy and Jeff had a really great time together, either in their lovemaking or their exciting discussions. The rest of the time, they were seldom in the same mood at the same time. Each was always trying to get the other to do things his or her way. This led to a great deal of fighting and finally to a state of truce as each decided to keep a certain distance from the other.

They have had sporadic marriage counseling for seven years and are still battling it out.

PERSONAL LOVE PROFILE

Number of Low Scores on
Emotional Maturity Rating
Form (EMRF)

Romantic Attraction
Questionnaire (RAQ) Score

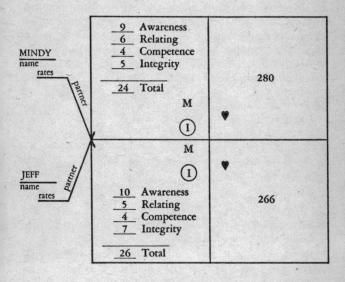

LOVE RELATIONSHIP TYPE_____3_____

Number of low EMRF Scores		*RAQ Scores*
0–20 low scores total	M	♥ 220–300 strong attraction
21 or more low scores total	I	♥ 200–220 borderline
		♡ 180–200 weak attraction

Types of Love Relationships

Type 1 ♥ M ♥ M	Type 4 ♥ M ♡ M	Type 7 ♡ M ♡ M
Type 2 ♥ M ♥ I	⎡Type 5 ♥ M ♡ I⎤	Type 8 ♡ M ♡ I
	⎣Type 5 ♡ M ♥ I⎦	
Type 3 ♥ I ♥ I	Type 6 ♥ I ♡ I	Type 9 ♡ I ♡ I

Rx for the Type-Three Relationship

Type-Three couples have what it takes to become a Type-One couple. Because their romantic attraction for each other is mutually high, they shouldn't divorce. Instead, they need to invest the energy they now use fighting with each other in growing up and gaining their much-needed maturity. If a Type-Three couple works hard at improving their relationship, they will graduate to a Type-One relationship. It takes a lot of hard work, but it is a shame for those in a Type-Three relationship to stand still in the midst of misery when they can progress to happier heights.

Here are some tips for both lovers:

- Stop fighting
- Own up to your immature behavior; you're *both* somewhat immature.
- Instead of divorce, both of you should go for marriage counseling or therapy.
- Strive every day to become a more mature person. Make this your daily goal.
- Rerate your maturity every week, using the EMRF. The progress you see will encourage you to try for more.
- Use the Rx for Type-One couples.

Chapter Eight

♡　♡　♡

One-Way
Love

Type-Four Relationships: Unrequited Love

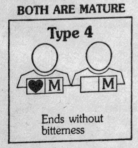

BOTH ARE MATURE

Type 4

Ends without bitterness

Type-Four relationships suffer one of the most common maladies ever read about or listened to in love songs, unrequited love. But Type Fours at least have the maturity to realize their relationship is one-sided romance. They move on to a new relationship with another person.

In the classical Type-Four case, both partners are mature, yet only one scores high on romantic attraction to the other. Because it is one-sided, the relationship doesn't work. The person who is romantically attracted suffers. A heart may be broken when a partner cannot reciprocate romantic feelings, but emotional maturity gives this person the resilience to overcome the disappointment and heartbreak.

185

Once partners in a Type-Four relationship see their disparate scores from the Romantic Attraction Questionnaire, they are secure enough and mature enough to realize that nothing can be done to make this match "work." Thus Type Fours will part as friends, but they probably will not see each other on a frequent basis, because for the person who *is* romantically involved, the association is a painful one. Both partners will go on to other relationships which will hopefully be mutual.

Can you fall in love with several different people?
Yes, you can. Potentially, there are a great many people with whom you can experience a high degree of romantic attraction. If you both have reasonably high emotional maturity and the other person is romantically attracted to you, then you have all the ingredients for a Type One relationship. There are many potentially great relationships, if only those who desire to have them make the effort to look. Invariably, the patients with whom I am successful say, "It's just like you said—numbers, numbers, numbers." The more people you get to know, the greater are your chances to have a relationship that has all the necessary elements. I am assuming here the willingness of you and your partner to work seriously on whatever maturity problems you have.

Few Type-Four Relationships Last

Most reasonably mature persons experience a Type-Four relationship sometime in their lives, perhaps several. But Type-Four couples don't belong together and eventually realize it. As a result, there aren't many Type-Four marriages. Those few couples who do marry, rarely stay together for any length of time.

From Type-Four to a Type-One Relationship

The Type-Four love affair is a difficult relationship to understand by lovers who are enmeshed in it. Only later, when they are in other relationships or married to other people, can they look back and see what happened.

Sue was very much attracted to Rob and very much wanted to marry him. Rob was a good boyfriend to Sue—attentive, kind, generous, and caring—but Sue knew that something for him was missing. They had been dating regularly for almost two years, but never more frequently than once a week. She wanted to move in with him and thought that their living together would increase his romantic responses and then they would marry.

Actually, Rob had only low romantic feelings for Sue. He liked her more than anyone else he had met, but he knew that he was not in love with her. Although he liked and respected Sue tremendously, she was not the girl of his dreams. With a divorce behind him already, Rob didn't want to make a second mistake.

Rob rated his romantic attraction for Sue at 182. When Sue met Lee and realized they were mutually attracted (he rated her at 283 on the RAQ), she realized the difference in the two relationships and told Rob she would not see him anymore. Rob was relieved and felt no reason to stop her from going on to another romance that might make her happier. Sue and Lee had a Type-One relationship. She felt some regret for having spent two years dating Rob and waiting for him to reciprocate her degree of interest. If Rob's score on the RAQ had been about 220, they would have had a Type-One relationship and of course both would have wanted to stay together.

PERSONAL LOVE PROFILE

Number of Low Scores on
Emotional Maturity Rating
Form (EMRF)

Romantic Attraction
Questionnaire (RAQ) Score

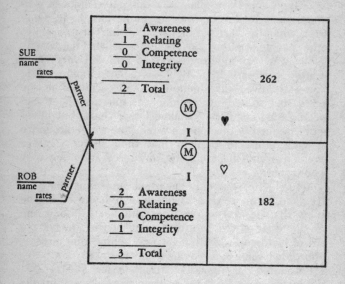

SUE
name
rates

partner

1	Awareness
1	Relating
0	Competence
0	Integrity
2	Total

Ⓜ

I

262

♥

ROB
name
rates

partner

Ⓜ

I

♡

2	Awareness
0	Relating
0	Competence
1	Integrity
3	Total

182

LOVE RELATIONSHIP TYPE _____ 4 _____

Number of low EMRF Scores

0–20 low scores total   M
21 or more low scores total   I

RAQ Scores

♥ 220–300 strong attraction
❤ 200–220 borderline
♡ 180–200 weak attraction

Types of Love Relationships

Type 1 ♥ M ♥ M	Type 4 ♥ M ♡ M	Type 7 ♡ M ♡ M
Type 2 ♥ M ♥ I	[Type 5 ♥ M ♡ I]	Type 8 ♡ M ♡ I
Type 3 ♥ I ♥ I	[Type 5 ♡ M ♥ I]	Type 9 ♡ I ♡ I
	Type 6 ♥ I ♡ I	

PERSONAL LOVE PROFILE

Number of Low Scores on
Emotional Maturity Rating
Form (EMRF)

Romantic Attraction
Questionnaire (RAQ) Score

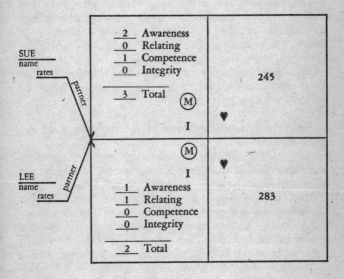

LOVE RELATIONSHIP TYPE_____1_____

Number of low EMRF Scores	*RAQ Scores*
0–20 low scores total M	♥ 220–300 strong attraction
21 or more low scores total I	♥ 200–220 borderline
	♡ 180–200 weak attraction

Types of Love Relationships

Type 1 ♥ M ♥ M	Type 4 ♥ M ♡ M	Type 7 ♡ M ♡ M
Type 2 ♥ M ♥ I	[Type 5 ♥ M ♡ I]	Type 8 ♡ M ♡ I
Type 3 ♥ I ♥ I	[Type 5 ♥ M ♥ I]	Type 9 ♡ I ♡ I
	Type 6 ♥ I ♡ I	

The Type-Four Breakup

When a Type-Four couple breaks up, typically one partner in the match (the one who is not in love) feels relief. The one who is in love goes through a period of depression but recovers in a short period of time. (How quickly he or she recovers is actually a function of emotional maturity. Stable people can roll with the punches, even the romantic ones.)

Type Fours are very resourceful and they realize that they are not meant for each other. They each move on to look for new partners.

Do men have better luck in finding new partners than women do?

Yes. It is unfair that population-wise there are more women available than men. It is a matter of supply and demand. And believe it or not, some locations have better ratios of men to women than other locations. For instance, the last census of Washington, D.C., indicated a ratio of about six women to one man. (If you are really interested in finding out about a specific town or city, write to the Bureau of Census, Washington, D.C.)

Another factor in the man's favor is that it is considered more socially acceptable for a man to actively look for a woman. Women are usually more sensitive and feel the need to be more subtle. They don't as often announce to their friends that they're anxious to meet a new man.

Type Fours' Quandary

If Type Fours happen to marry, eventually they face a quandary that could be clarified by using The Love Test. It is then easy to see that they are not suffering from neurosis. They are confused because they have chosen the wrong person.

"I like you so much. What's wrong with me that I'm not happy?"

"I like you and trust you. Why do I feel that something is missing?"

"I really like you a lot, but I don't have the kind of feelings I had toward my old boyfriend."

"Is there something wrong with me that I can't make this marriage work?"

Since Type-Four partners have no significant problems of maturity, they have a need to search within themselves for the probable romantic reason why the relationship is not more fulfilling. *Nothing* can make a Type-Four relationship work better. They don't need to ask, "Is there something wrong with *Me*?" With such unmatched RAQ scores, the couple suffers from one-way love. Type Fours can end their problems by separating and finding new partners with whom their RAQ's are mutually high.

Rejection Hurts

Despite the fact that the lovers in a Type-Four situation are mature, the one who is rejected is going to have hurt feelings upon discovering that those feelings of romantic attraction are not mutual. This partner will recover, and will be thankful to have learned the truth, but he or she will suffer some pain. Despite the emotional trauma, the partner will recover.

The Love Test system is primarily intended to help lovers avoid divorce by preventing unsuitable matches in the first place. It is better to suffer three months of hurt when learning to live with the truth of a one-way love affair than to marry and live together in misery for many years and eventually divorce.

Very often the person who is romantically attracted knows deep in his or her heart that those romantic feelings are not mutual, but since one of them is enjoying the relationship, that person wants to continue the relationship. After a period of time, when the person who is attracted wants a commitment and none is forthcoming, the couple is likely to face up to the fact that they are simply not right for each other.

When the lover who is saddened by the breakup sees the RAQ scores, he or she is better able to recognize and admit that the affair would never have been fulfilling. The Type-Four lover who is involved in the relationship but who is not highly attracted to the other partner may be reluctant to use The Love Test materials, for fear of hurting his or her friend's feelings. Although such consideration is commendable, it is more important that the truth of the relationship be unveiled for what it is so that both lovers can move on to romances where there is mutual romantic attraction. The lover who is suffering from unrequited love will recover.

Protecting the Ego of the Rejected Partner

The Love Test is primarily intended to serve as a preventive tool, to prevent divorce by discouraging unsuitable partners from marrying in the first place. When The Love Test is used to help study a marriage that already exists, the RAQ and EMRF scores may lead to serious questioning about whether the marriage should continue or be dissolved.

There are many partners who choose to stay together despite low ratings on The Love Test materials; a marital relationship can be built on many things beside romantic attraction. A separation is never recommended on the basis of RAQ scores alone; the total picture must be taken into account.

Should the couple decide to separate, the partner who feels strong romantic attraction for his or her spouse will suffer not only the grief of separation from a lover but also the very heavy blow of rejection. Both partners may also feel a sense of guilt or failure about the dissolution of their marriage. Here are some suggestions to help ease the emotional adjustment of such a separation:

- Each partner should reassure the other that neither one has wronged the other. They simply made a mistake, especially common to young people, of choosing their life partners before they had enough information, experience, and wisdom. Neither partner is evil; neither partner is guilty; and neither partner should look upon this separation as a punishment.

- The romantically attracted partner should be given a large dose of approval to counteract any feeling of "failure." Marriage is not a test to be passed or flunked. Both partners, with the best of intentions and hopes, entered into this marriage. The marriage was a mistake, but the partners are okay people.

- Joint counseling is recommended to be sure that it is not a fear problem that underlies the one low RAQ rating. Therapy can help solve a fear problem that blankets an underlying strong romantic attraction. The partner who is leaving should be honest in saying that even though the relationship can never be one of romantic love, he or she would like to remain on friendly terms, if mutually agreeable.

- The separation should be viewed as an opportunity for *both* partners to find new and satisfying relationships based on mutual romantic attraction.

- The partner who is leaving should call upon his or her emotional maturity and demonstrate a sense of fairness, decency, and generosity by avoiding bitter struggles over division of financial assets, "first rights" to mutual friends, and the legal and physical custody of the children.

Rx for Type-Four Relationships

The Type-Four relationship is usually short and unful-
filling because one of the partners suffers from a lack of
romantic interest. There are two possible directions for
a Type-Four relationship to go, so RAQ scores will
definitely influence the final outcome.

- If the partner with the weak romantic interest has
  very low RAQ scores, the couple should part as
  friends and look for new partners who can share
  mutual attraction. It is unlikely that this Type-Four
  couple is already married and this is the perfect
  example of preventing divorce by not marrying the
  wrong partner. With other partners with whom these
  mature people share high romantic attraction, they
  can have Type-One relationships. While a breakup
  may be upsetting at first, these people are emotionally
  strong and will bounce back quickly. Type Fours have
  the ability to be happier with someone else.

- If the partner with the low romantic interest has a
  borderline feeling (200 to 220 score on the RAQ), the
  partners should remain together and follow the prescription for a Type-One relationship by upgrading
  the few maturity areas where there is room for
  improvement. The good things going for this relationship should be appreciated; they probably override
  the fact that one person's romantic attraction is not all
  that strong. This Type-Four couple can be happy
  together.

Type Fives: Mismatched and Miserable

Life isn't easy for the Type-Five couple because Type Fives have *two* problems and they exist in the relationship in *two* different ways! They suffer from one-sided love and immaturity in one of the partners.

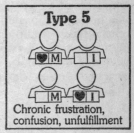

ONE IS MATURE

Chronic frustration, confusion, unfulfillment

These *two* problems can be in any of four possible arrangements, with both problems in one person or with each of the lovers having one of the problems.

Without The Love Test materials to make a diagnosis, it's hard to figure out just what's going on with most Type-Five relationships. Even when The Love Test evaluations give us a clear picture of what is wrong, it's not always easy to come to a fully satisfactory resolution. Often trade-offs, compromises, and a great deal of acceptance are called for.

Type Five is the most complex of all the relationships. And about one third of the population of the United States, if my practice and classes are at all representative, suffer from this type of double trouble.

There is the possibility that some Type-Five couples can work things out and live reasonably happily. This can happen if the one with the lower RAQ has a borderline score, or if the one with the immaturity problem has only borderline immaturity (not much more than 21 low EMRF scores).

In classic Type-Five relationships, one partner suffers from considerable emotional immaturity and one of the partners has weak romantic interest. However, both of these problems may exist in the same mate. Without help, the couple either will remain confused and unhappily together or split up and wander around wondering what went wrong.

It is not uncommon for Type-Five couples to stay unhappily married: They may be waiting for the kids to grow up; they may be hiding their discomfort; they may have love affairs outside of the marriage; but they often stay in the relationship "till death do them part." They remain together out of a medley of one person's romantic interest, one person's caring treatment, a moderate degree of uncertainty, and reluctance to change on the part of the one who is less mature, more fearful of change.

We Thought We Were Happy

There are some Type-Five relationships in which the couple appears to be quite content with their lives together. Remember Stan (see pp. 16–18)? He believed his life with Michelle was happy enough until he met Kim.

Type Fives are usually an accident waiting to happen. Type Fives are often bound together in marriages of confusion because the partner with the low romantic attraction for his or her mate has not yet met Mr. or Ms. Right and is a romantic virgin. He or she suffers the effects of immaturity problems. Perhaps through The Love Test the immature person comes to understand the problem and gets help. They may agree to hold their marriage together because they *want* to stay together rather than keeping it simply because of denial, confusion, and dependency. They don't know about a Type-One relationship because they have never experienced it, so they don't consciously yearn for another type of relationship. They can go through life and marriage somewhat comfortably—as long as they never meet the person with whom they will share high romantic attraction.

Or they may split up, realizing that they will never be happily married and that apart they have a much better chance for being happier with another partner. When the partners in a Type-Five relationship separate, the immature partner may grow up and find better relationships with other partners. Then each person has a better chance at being happy, provided the immature one becomes determined to grow up.

If the RAQ score for either partner is below 180, no matter what the emotional maturity scores and who has to get help in growing up, the Type-Five couple will not find the fulfillment that exists in a mutually romantic relationship.

Should You Split?

Leaving a marriage, even a bad one, is frightening and threatening to most people, and they will be inclined to reject any information that suggests they *need* to divorce.

Certainly, the point of this book is to tell you not to get a divorce, unless there is absolutely no other reasonable alternative.

One of the principal problems found in Type-Five couples is that the partners married in haste. While they are living in the same house in a state of truce, they may suspect, deep within their souls, that they didn't take the chance or allow sufficient time to look for a person with whom they had a mutually high romantic attraction.

If you have rated yourself to be in a Type-Five relationship, you may be tempted to seek a divorce. However, before you call a lawyer, you owe it to yourself to take an inventory of the benefits of your marriage. There may be many assets that you haven't taken the time to assess properly, and haven't yet put romantic attraction and maturity problems into a deservedly broad enough context. You owe it to yourself and your partner to assess your relationship with the added perspective of the seven benefits of marriage described below.

Assessing the Benefits of a Marriage Relationship

People marry for many reasons, and many combinations of reasons. In order to get a better understanding of what benefits you *are* enjoying from your marriage and what price you are paying for these benefits, let's look at the usual reasons people marry and see if we can find your benefit/cost ratio.

It is important for you to remember two things:

1. Nobody has a perfect marriage.
2. Everything in life has its price.

What's important is that you feel right about the price. Keep this in mind as you consider the reasons you married and your own benefits and costs in keeping your relationship going.

Benefits of Marriage

Companionship

Eating, sleeping, and waking up together, and just sharing the everyday interests of life are more enjoyable and more meaningful than experiencing these things alone. If being alone were as pleasurable as being together, then long ago our ancestors would have wandered off each by himself, and there would have been no tribes, no nuclear families, no lovers, and none of us would be here today. Being together feels much better. That is our heritage and our destiny.

Belonging for Mutual Aid

It is undeniable that there is safety, security, and strength in numbers. We are all safer and more secure in the typical family structure. If there is danger or a problem to be solved, the more people to deal with it, the better is the chance for success. This is not basically the social need for companionship; this is a requirement that enhances our chances of survival. We feel best and function best when we know that we have the acceptance and protective interest of another person and of the larger group. This security gives us the insurance that we need against all the challenges, threats, and dangers to our survival. Marriage throughout all cultures has been the basic bulwark against the scary business of going it alone.

Basic Emotional Needs

No one will be content unless his basic emotional needs are met. For a meaningful and satisfying life, we need to be a productive, contributing person. This we can be with or without a marriage partner. But our second need for a meaningful and satisfying life is to have a fairly regular diet of attention, approval, and affection. If we do not have a life partner, then how can we expect to get these needs met? These needs are met only irregularly at work. Friends or relatives give us more, but for the physical and spiritual affection we all need, there is nothing better than a caring lover.

Sex

For most of us, the absolutely peak experience in life is the sexual fulfillment that we have with a loving partner. And when we have this kind of satisfying sex on a regular (not compulsive) basis, then almost everything in life seems to go more smoothly, and we have a much more positive outlook. We need sex to feel our best and function at our best, and masturbation, for all its popularity, can never compete with sex with a partner, especially a loving partner. There is just no comparison.

Sex, outside the framework of a meaningful relationship, is just that. It can satisfy for a little while, but for almost all of us it leaves the uneasy feeling that we are not solidly anchored in the world, that each new day we must go out and try to get our sexual needs met in chancy and uncertain ways, absent of the security that only marriage can give.

Interaction

When we have someone to interact with, we have much better reality-testing. It is well known that hermits and recluses gradually lose touch with reality. Experiments at McGill University showed that, if we are deprived of the ordinary environmental stimulation of sight and sound and movement, within twenty-four hours most people become totally disoriented, hallucinatory, and delusional. We need stimulation and the interest of another person, and this is provided in the most reliable possible way through marriage.

Another aspect of interaction is the excitement marriage provides. Life is just more interesting and more varied when we have an enjoyable companion with whom to share our grandiose ideas, mundane discussions, daily problems, new experiences, large failures, and little joys. Through our companions, we have intimate access to two lives rather than just one.

Interaction as stimulation and excitement is most reliably provided by a loving companion who is, at the same time, your marital partner.

Financial Benefits

It is a simple fact of life that two can live more cheaply than one. And if there is a sharp division of responsibilities, with only one wage earner, then a deep and abiding trust should exist, with the commitment to the nonearning partner that proper financial obligations will be fulfilled.

Parenthood

For all the advantages of birth control, birth statistics are on the rise. Many who deferred having children in their twenties are now eager to have children in their thirties. Children enrich our lives by giving us the chance to teach and to wisely guide, an opportunity to extend our own learning and growth, and the appreciation and pride that can only come from watching a loved child grow into adulthood. Being a single parent can work, but raising a child is a task much more difficult for one than for two, except when the second partner is a very immature person who contributes more trouble than help.

Each one of us who is married receives these benefits to a certain extent. If the benefits are great, and mutual, then neither partner will be interested in splitting up. It's just too much to give up, and there would be no reason to. But in less fulfilling marriages, there could be less reason to stay together, especially if the price is just too high for the few benefits received. There are some marriages where there are so few benefits and so much pain that no one would question the wisdom of divorce.

As we've already seen, people marry for a variety of reasons; many of them are not good reasons and many of these marriages may end in divorce. Those who marry to "belong" to someone, who are afraid of being "old maids," who are primarily after financial security, social status, and escape from home, convenient sex, or any of a hundred other reasons, will find that they're going to pay a heavy price for this kind of devil's bargain.

But what about that broad middle ground, where the benefits in a relationship are not so great, but they are still "pretty good"? How can we determine if the benefits are really worth the cost?

Your first step should be to sit down with your spouse and discuss these seven benefits in order to determine whether your relationship supplies these benefits for each of you. If your degree of mutual romantic attraction is borderline or more (both have scores of about 200 or better, based on a number of ratings, not simply a single rating), then emotional immaturity is almost certainly the underlying cause of your marital dissatisfactions. This means that there is plenty of hope for your relationship.

If you each make and keep a commitment to use the methods for bringing out the best in each other, your relationship will certainly improve, and as it does the benefit/cost ratio will automatically improve accordingly. You will have wisely decided to stay together, and will have launched a program to insure that you will not only stay together but that the relationship will become more and more fulfilling for both of you.

If your romantic attraction scores show one person to have a consistently low score (in the 180 range), and the other partner to score above 200, then you will be in for some serious and difficult decision making.

Assessing the Benefit/Cost Ratio

The word *divorce* is terrifying to most people. Divorce implies a complete undermining of marital security; the loss of that reliable companionship, mutual aid, fulfillment of emotional needs, sex, interaction, financial partnership, and help in parenting that marriage provides.

Making a list, such as the example that follows, will help you a great deal to clarify your thoughts and feelings.

ILLUSTRATIVE EXAMPLE OF BENEFIT/COST RATIO
Stan's relationship with his wife, Michelle:

Need	Benefits Received	Cost or Price Paid
Companionship	Low: Uninteresting only having another person around Moderately high: Lessens guilt feeling	High: Time away from Kim High: If divorce, because there is so much guilt
Belonging for Mutual Aid	High: Michelle is a devoted wife and mother	High: Time away from Kim, a much more desired partner
Basic Emotional Needs	Low: Attention, acceptance, approval, and affection not wanted; unfulfilling	High: Getting these needs met by Kim not possible if marriage continues
Sex	Low: Unfulfilling	High: Much more preferable with Kim
Interaction	Low: Not a very stimulating partner	High: Being away from a very stimulating partner
Parenthood	High: Be with children every day; not have to pay for divorce, spousal and child support	High: Expensive, but lowered by the fact that Kim earns a good salary to supplement income

The overall picture shows why Stan decided to get a divorce, finally. The benefits showed a mixed to low picture, but the costs of remaining married (in emotional and financial terms) were felt to be very high—too high for Stan.

Need	Benefits Received	Cost or Price Paid
Companionship	_____	_____
Belonging for Mutual Aid	_____	_____
Basic Emotional Needs	_____	_____
Sex	_____	_____
Interaction	_____	_____
Financial Benefits	_____	_____
Parenthood	_____	_____

You should use at least one sheet of paper to list your benefits and the price you feel you are paying in each category. Your mood of the moment will influence how positively or negatively you picture each benefit and each price, but this can be reasonably objectified by making repeated ratings. Over a period of time, you will see a clear and sharp picture emerging. You will find it easier to be honest with yourself about what you do and don't have, and to what extent you believe your relationship is something of value, something worth working hard to keep and improve.

If you conclude that you have been receiving minimal benefits at an unreasonable price, then your decision will have fallen into place for you. After a thorough discussion with your partner, and cross-checking with a professional, you can be sure of what you want to do and why you have chosen to end a relationship for which you can see no hope.

If you were happily married and then discovered that your partner once had an affair but it's over now, what should you do? Is this a reason to get divorced?

To divorce because of an extramarital affair wou[ld]
to divorce for the wrong reason. Having an affai[r]
symptom of something more basic, something that should
be identified and understood. There can be many reasons for having an extramarital affair and you need to
learn the underlying cause before you decide to divorce.

The mature partner in a Type-Two relationship may
have affairs because he or she is antagonized by the
immature partner. The mature partner frequently becomes frustrated and disappointed and figures, "The
hell with you. I'll go out to find someone easier to be
with." The partner is not after sex; he or she is searching for some emotionally fulfilling involvement.

Meanwhile, it is likely that the *immature* partner is
motivated to have an affair to "prove" acceptability,
indulge in an ego trip, or dilute the emotional investment he or she has in the spouse (another example of
the moth-and-flame syndrome).

Type-Three couples are apt to have affairs because
they are immature and really don't understand how to
develop healthy human relationships. Therefore, they
quest blindly for good treatment or try to bolster sag-
ging egos. They may also have affairs out of revenge
because they get a neurotic satisfaction out of hurting their
partners. They can either get revenge secretly or they
may tell their partners about the affairs for the purpose
of hurting them. Sometimes this is done under the
guise of "valuing honesty above all else." I have never
seen this kind of confession do any good, and almost
always have seen it do irreparable harm.

Type Fives have so many problems going on that it
depends on where the hearts (RAQ scores) are in each
couple's diagram. But there are many strong possibilities for extramarital affairs here. The person with low
romantic interest may have affairs because he or she
feels that something is missing. The immature person
may have an affair because he or she feels that something is missing (emotional closeness), and is acting out
his or her immaturity. What's really missing is the

maturity that could allow the spouse's love to be recognized and felt.

When something is missing, the immature person may try many different ways of getting what's missing. Immature people are likely to become alcoholics, workaholics, or have several love affairs at the same time or in close, consecutive order. The immature partner is capable of acting out in many strange ways because he or she doesn't know what the basic problem really is.

What if *only one* partner wants to end the relationship? At this point marriage counseling is always indicated. A surprising number of people say that they regret having ended a relationship. These couples admit there were problems, but after seeing what has happened in the relationships that followed, they realize that they jumped out too quickly, and later wish that they had made a more devoted effort to improve their initial relationship. A counselor can help couples to make those constructive efforts to improve a relationship. (If, by chance, you have skipped p. 192, go back and read the section, "Protecting the Ego of the Rejected Partner.")

Does age have anything to do with selection of a mate?

Frequently, but not always. Around twenty years old the overriding determinants in a relationship are romantic attraction and the sexual needs of the man. Insecurity often figures prominently on the woman's part; she may be afraid that if she doesn't marry the man who's asking her now, she will never get another chance. Research shows that before living together became popular, almost half of all marriages involved a teen-age girl (reported by Ray Short in 1978).

By age forty, both men and women have an entirely different set of motivations. The desire for romantic attraction is still there, but the difference is that the forty-year-old has a great deal of experience, and experience tends to increase maturity. He or she has been buffeted around enough to have had plenty of both

pleasure and pain. He or she knows that even t.
romance and sex are exciting, there's more to a d.
relationship. The forty-year-old is much more sophist
cated, aware, and experienced, and knows that the
most important things are companionship and caring for
another person.

Past age sixty, people are principally concerned with
companionship—finding a person who is affectionate,
interesting, and easygoing. Sexual interest is there, but
it's not nearly as strong as it was at age twenty.

Age differences between partners can be a matter of
trade-offs. I've seen couples in which the man was as
much as ten, twenty, or twenty-five years older than
the woman and the relationships have worked out very
well if there was a high mutual romantic attraction. I
have also seen couples in which the man was married to
a woman ten years older, and many of these relationships also worked out well. The principal factor, more
important than the age difference, was whether these
people enjoyed each other and delighted in each other's
company. "Thrilling" is a two-way street. If both people
are excited about each other, they can live happily
together.

*Just why do people get married—especially in these
days when living together is okay?*

While romance is a very powerful drive, we all need
security too. Even people who love adventurous activities still want to have a secure relationship. When
people know what they are doing and why, marriage
means a commitment forever—for better or for worse,
in sickness and in health. People in Type-One relationships marry because they feel so lucky and wish to
document and secure the relationship.

The Toxic Relationship versus the Nourishing Relationship

Romantic attraction is the main motivating force in making and sustaining a relationship, but the quality of a relationship depends upon the caring that a lover recieves from the other partner. The ability to be a caring partner is rooted in a person's emotional maturity. Some people connect with "nourishing" lovers who provide warm, caring, comfortable, and growing relationships. Other people become entangled with inconsiderate, "toxic" lovers who are rude and demeaning, maybe even cruel.

Dr. Jerry A. Greenwald identified these two types of people, and he contends that each person is responsible for the kind of treatment he gets from another person because each person has the choice of staying in or ending a relationship. The more mature you are, the more you are able to judge sensibly the kind of treatment you are getting and decide if this treatment makes you happy or not. Mature people know they are worthy of a lover who is kind. Immature people have doubts about their own self-worth and may subject themselves to lovers who are rude and unkind because they think they don't deserve anything better.

The mature person will tend to seek a mature lover.

The immature person is more likely to end up with an immature lover.

Sometimes the immature person will be lucky and attract a mature lover, and the mature lover will help the immature person to become more mature.

Compare these traits:

Mature (*nourishing*) Lover	Immature (*toxic*) Lover
Has self-awareness	Lacks self-awareness
Has high self-esteem	Has low self-esteem
Has integrity	Is insincere

Mature (*nourishing*) Lover	Immature (*toxic*)
Helps others	Is a taker, not a gi
Is flexible	Is inflexible
Is self-sufficient	Is dependent on oth
Gives compliments	Is unappreciative
Is optimistic	Is pessimistic
Communicates well	Doesn't listen to others
Is compassionate and understanding	Thinks only of self

If the toxic person gets professional help, maturity can improve and nourishing behavior will begin to appear. When paired with a loving and mature partner as well as a good counselor, the toxic person will grow up even faster. If a toxic person refuses help, he or she will never change. Despite promises to change, many immature people are just not mature enough to help themselves without a caring lover or professional guidance.

The High Cost of a Toxic Relationship

Life with a toxic person is very costly. Everything in life has its price; the price may not be financial, it could be emotional. Sacrifices and compromises are part of the price of any relationship.

In many toxic relationships, however, only one partner is doing the giving, the compromising, and the sacrificing. This ultimately leads to frustration, anger, and unhappiness. The ratio between the reward and the frustration is grossly out of line and chronic frustration becomes a way of life. The price of being together becomes very steep. Sometimes a person is driven by such a great deal of romantic attraction for the toxic partner that he or she is willing to pay a very high price. As the price becomes too great to bear, chronic frustration sets in. In time, the loving partner will demand to get something back. If still nothing comes, ultimately the loving partner will want to end the relationship.

After all, kindness is paramount in a relationship. If you are not being treated kindly, you can ask your partner to try to do better or you can say good-bye. Your unkind lover may force you into a corner where you must continue to be emotionally beaten and bruised, or you must make the difficult decision to leave the relationship. Only you can decide what price you are willing to pay to maintain your current relationship.

The Type-Five Fates

Couples who have borderline Type-Five/Type-Two relationships should seek professional help and work at saving their relationship.

Couples who are classic Type Fives should also seek professional advice. Remember, however, that therapy is particularly essential for the immature partner if he or she is to go on to another more promising relationship.

Seeking Help

Often someone will come in to see me and say that his or her partner wouldn't come along. The partner's refusal to seek counseling should not be taken as proof that he or she doesn't want to work on the relationship. Your partner may be using some indirect communication, with or without being conscious of it. For example, your partner may honestly believe that because you both have done everything in your power that there is nothing more to be done. Your partner may, however, have a secret hope that something can be done. Your partner may be saying, "Okay, you go out and talk to that counselor, and if you can find out something that can convince me, then you come back and tell me about it. Prove to me that there is some hope. Then, if you're convincing, maybe I'll take a look at this vague stuff they call counseling."

Keep in mind what I tell almost every despairing couple that I work with. "I know that you feel there is not much hope for the relationship, but you came to this conclusion because you have exhausted all of your resourcefulness. I'd like you to start thinking that you haven't even begun to tap into my resources. And keep in mind that it's never too late to give up."

If you can see that there are still benefits to be gained from and hope for your relationship, then you shouldn't give up, even if your partner moves out.

As I've said, the typical sequence of events that I have seen is that one partner will come in first. Most often it is the wife, but sometimes it is the husband.

Carl, whose wife came in to see me first, illustrates a common dynamic. After the first seven visits by his wife, he appeared in the waiting room, a stranger to me, but obviously along for the visit with Lina. In Lina's presence, Carl delivered a twenty-minute discourse about psychology being "vague," about counselors being "unable to understand the really fine nuances of a relationship" and "having a tendency to meddle where they have no business meddling." It became apparent to me that he was not there to tell me how bad therapy is, but rather to learn indirectly what influence his wife was being subjected to. His purpose was to be able to counter such an "interfering" influence. Most astonishing was his admission in his next, private session, that, "I've always been an angry and insecure person, and I've had an outside hope that maybe you could help me do something about it."

It Might Not Be Over

If you are in a relationship that you want to keep, and your partner convinces you that he or she does not want to continue and moves out, stays out, and never calls or stops by for a month or two, your relationship still might not be over. You can be reasonably certain that, at least at this time, your partner probably *believes* that he or she wants out permanently. But remember that this feeling may or may not persist. I have seen many people who have moved out and then moved back in again. Any experienced therapist knows that there is always ambivalence—feeling *good* about some aspects of the relationship and *bad* about others. Mixed feelings are the rule for most every marital relationship. I have often seen a couple leave a session in a state of silent anger toward each other, only to reappear several days later in a jovial and mutually congenial mood.

The key point to remember is that there is always ambivalence, and as long as there is ambivalence there is hope. So don't give up; try everything that is available to you and leave open every chance for reconciliation.

However, it is unwise for you to go on hoping indefinitely, keeping your life on hold. If your partner shows no interest and is determined to end the relationship, then it is time to get on with your life. Keep in mind there are many members of the opposite sex who are as eager for the fulfillment of a good relationship as you are. Consider the various ways of meeting appropriate possible new partners, and take the initiative!

If your spouse or lover leaves you and then comes back to you, what should you do?

If your lover is willing, I mean seriously willing, to go with you for counseling, then take him or her back. If he or she won't go, or agrees but says he or she can't take the time, stop hoping. Your partner will leave you again some time in the future. People who refuse counseling almost never make good spouses, lovers, or partners. They are fighting help. What could be more hopeless?

Rx for Type-Five Relationships

Because Type-Five relationships have two problems it is wise for the Type-Five couple to sort out the costs and benefits of the relationship. Borderline Type Five/Type Twos have a reasonably good chance of a life-long, happy relationship. Classic Type-Five relationships are a lot more difficult. If an unmarried couple's Love Test indicates a Type-Five relationship, they would be wise to get a professional opinion before the wedding.

- Take your Personal Love Profile to a professional who can help you determine if you have a borderline Type-Five/Type-Two relationship. If so, do not separate but work at growing up.
- If you have a classic Type-Five relationship, determine the benefit/cost ratio and then reevaluate your situation.
- Practice the prescriptions for Type-One and Type-Two relationships.

Type-Six Relationships: Fated for Failure

A Type-Six love affair is like a Type-Four relationship—one partner suffers from unrequited love. But unlike Type Fours, the partners in this couple are immature. The person who *is* in love can't understand why the other partner doesn't give good treatment or enough attention. The person who is not in love just isn't invested in

NEITHER IS MATURE

Type 6

Fall apart, usually very soon, blaming each other

the relationship enough to care much about what happens. This partner is in the relationship for selfish reasons and does little to enrich the relationship. At the first hint of trouble, pressure, or involvement, he or she is out the door and running from trouble. The two lovers are really inadequate adults. They are lacking in resourcefulness; they both wish to be taken care of. Only one is romantically attracted to the other. Both are immature.

These three problems (one case of one-way love and two cases of immaturity) can lead a couple in two different directions: Some Type-Six relationships are brief love affairs or marriages that quickly fall apart, each partner blaming the other; other Type-Six relationships can last for many years because the relationship is held together by dependency. The partners feel like running from each other, but they are too scared to try to make it alone in the real world. Besides, deep inside they fear that no one else would want them.

When Both Lovers Are Toxic

If you know the manifestations of one toxic lover (see pp. 208–210, imagine what happens when *two* toxic lovers get together. Add the fact that only one of them has a high degree of romantic attraction for the other. The result is obvious disaster, a short-lived romance with either no future at all or a painfully long future of misery, frustration, and resentment.

The day after his marriage to Laura, Matt found himself inexplicably cut off from his wife. Only two days before the wedding, everything seemed fine. But after the ceremony, a dramatic change came over Laura.

"I'm in love with her, but her love for me has disappeared," he told me, searching for a way to make Laura more responsive to him. "First she was warm and loving, then we got married and suddenly she's an iceberg."

Laura, on the other hand, couldn't understand why Matt didn't make her happy. After all, he said he loved her. It was his job to make sure she was happy.

The Romantic Attraction Questionnaire showed that while Matt felt strong romantic interest in Laura, she felt little toward him. She mainly wanted him to take care of her. Both scored quite low in the emotional maturity ratings, showing little awareness or ability to relate well to others. Matt, however, was relatively high on integrity while Laura scored extremely low on self-discipline. Her overall functioning in life, her involvement with the world around her, was marginal. She had been taken care of all her life and expected Matt to continue where her parents had left off.

As time went on, Matt accused Laura of not trying and not working at their relationship. Laura retaliated by whining that Matt was impatient with her. She blamed him for "rushing her into marriage" and finally lashed out at him for "getting involved with another woman," which wasn't true.

Matt had just enough insight to realize that it was an impossible situation and that he and Laura would never have a happy relationship. As Matt came to this conclusion and found strength, Laura retreated more and more into her shell. He felt relieved when she finally asked for a divorce from this "terribly demanding man" and went to live with an aunt.

Matt spent some time in counseling trying to figure out what had been wrong; he was determined to learn from the mistakes he had made. He improved his own maturity to the point where he was ready to seek a new relationship, this time with a mature woman, not a little girl disguised as a woman.

Kate and Jack are now in their late fifties. Both grew up in impoverished homes. Kate's father deserted the family soon after she was born. Her mother, with a limited education, struggled to survive and support her daughter by taking menial jobs. Kate suffered largely from neglect. Nobody ever told her or showed her what life was about. She was shy and suffered from a sense of being very different and very inferior. She never had any close friends.

Jack's father was an alcoholic who was abusive to and neglectful of his children. Jack grew up angry, hating his father, himself, school, and the world in general.

Soon after high school, Kate met Jack. Both had limited dating experience. Kate worked in a laundry and kept mostly to herself. Jack drove a delivery truck. When he met Kate at work, he found her romantically

PERSONAL LOVE PROFILE

Number of Low Scores on
Emotional Maturity Rating
Form (EMRF)

Romantic Attraction
Questionnaire (RAQ) Score

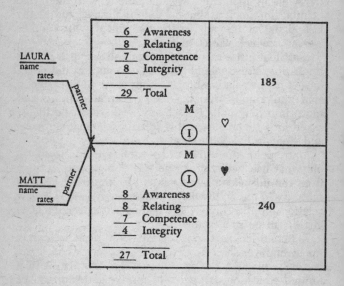

LAURA
name
rates

partner

6	Awareness
8	Relating
7	Competence
8	Integrity
29	Total

M

Ⓘ

185   ♡

MATT
name
rates

partner

M

Ⓘ

♥

8	Awareness
8	Relating
7	Competence
4	Integrity
27	Total

240

LOVE RELATIONSHIP TYPE _____ 6 _____

Number of low EMRF Scores

0–20 low scores total   M
21 or more low scores total   I

RAQ Scores

♥ 220–300 strong attraction
♥ 200–220 borderline
♡ 180–200 weak attraction

Types of Love Relationships

Type 1 ♥ M ♥ M	Type 4 ♥ M ♡ M	Type 7 ♡ M ♡ M
Type 2 ♥ M ♥ I	[Type 5 ♥ M ♡ I]	Type 8 ♡ M ♡ I
	[Type 5 ♡ M ♥ I]	
Type 3 ♥ I ♥ I	Type 6 ♥ I ♡ I	Type 9 ♡ I ♡ I

exciting. She wasn't romantically interested in Jack, but she was flattered that someone would take an interest in her. When he proposed, she quickly accepted.

Jack's frustrations in dealing with people and his low self-esteem led him to copy his father's drinking pattern. While romantically in love with Kate, he never treated her very well. Neither one of them had much insight into his or her own needs or the impediments to their really growing up.

Neither really had a chance. Inevitably, they brought out the worst in each other, but hung very closely together because they were close to no one else and were afraid of the big, uncertain world out there. As the years ticked by, their mutual sense of bitterness became more and more entrenched. They remained unhappily together because they lacked the resourcefulness to do something to improve their lot in life.

Type-Six couples suffer from two kinds of problems: Not only must one partner deal with unrequited love, but each must cope with the other's and his or her own immature behavior. The Type-Six relationship often goes on for years, possibly even a lifetime, while the partners bog down each other with their mutual morbid dependency and their inability to work at their situation. With professional help, they can grow up enough to see two clear choices: They may gain the maturity it takes to separate and find other partners to whom they are better suited, or they can grow up and discover the benefits of their improved, mature treatment of each other. Once the partners in a Type-Six relationship gain some maturity, they will be happier people.

Rx for Type-Six Relationships

- Take your Love Test scores for a professional opinion and get help in determining how accurate your ratings are.
- Make a determined commitment to upgrade both partners' maturity; this is your key to happiness.

PERSONAL LOVE PROFILE

Number of Low Scores on
Emotional Maturity Rating
Form (EMRF)

Romantic Attraction
Questionnaire (RAQ) Score

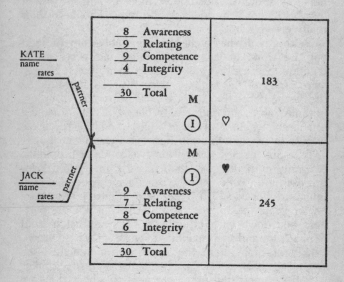

KATE
name
rates
partner

8	Awareness
9	Relating
9	Competence
4	Integrity
30	Total

M
(I)

183 ♡

JACK
name
rates
partner

M
(I)

♥

9	Awareness
7	Relating
8	Competence
6	Integrity
30	Total

245

LOVE RELATIONSHIP TYPE _____ 6 _____

Number of low EMRF Scores
0–20 low scores total   M
21 or more low scores total I

RAQ Scores
♥ 220–300 strong attraction
♥ 200–220 borderline
♡ 180–200 weak attraction

Types of Love Relationships

Type 1 ♥ M ♥ M   Type 4 ♥ M ♡ M   Type 7 ♡ M ♡ M

Type 2 ♥ M ♥ I   [Type 5 ♥ M ♡ I]
[Type 5 ♡ M ♥ I]   Type 8 ♡ M ♡ I

Type 3 ♥ I ♥ I   Type 6 ♥ I ♡ I   Type 9 ♡ I ♡ I

- As you become more mature, rerate each other on both romantic attraction and emotional maturity. You may have progressed to a Type-Four relationship.
- Follow the prescriptions for Type-One and Type-Two couples.

Chapter Nine

♡ ♡ ♡

No-Way
Love

Love is not easy for the couples in Type-Seven, -Eight or -Nine relationships. They don't have romantic attraction on their side, so no matter how mature they may or may not be, they will not find real happiness together. *If* the mature people in these relationships can connect with someone to whom they are romantically attracted and who is attracted to them, they *do* have the chance to form a Type-One relationship. Both of the people in Type-Seven, -Eight, and -Nine relationships have connected with the wrong persons. These people should look for other partners who can supply the missing romantic interest.

Immature people in Type-Eight and -Nine relationships need to improve their emotional maturity—and find a new partner—before they can have a happy love relationship.

Type-Seven Relationships: The Possibility of Friendship

Type Sevens have an unful-filling, but not unhappy, rela-tionship. Once they understand that romance is missing, they can end up the best of friends for life. They can remain friends because Type-Seven couples are both mature. They just don't have a high enough romantic attraction to make for a deeply satisfying love. They like each

BOTH MATURE

Type 7

Falls apart very soon, without any bitterness

other, they respect each other, and they probably have many things in common. They may marry and have a very settled, passionless kind of relationship. More than likely, before they get to the altar, they will realize they just weren't meant for each other.

Do you need a love relationship to be a happy person?

No, but research shows there's a much higher correla-tion between a happy love life and personal happiness than how far up the corporate ladder you advance. Also, happily married people tend to live longer and to be healthier than single people.

On the other hand, you can be legally married and be so uninvolved with your partner that you really aren't married at all (see p. 131). There are some people who are "married" to their work or their hobbies. Everyone who has a passion about something has a greater chance of being happy. That passion may not be another human being.

"All I know is that something's wrong between Bill and me," Angela wailed when we first met.

Bill agreed with Angela that there was a problem

and, though they both sensed that something was wrong, they were unable to define it. They never fought. They had many friends and interests in common. They liked and respected each other and were even involved in a joint business venture. Each found in the other qualities he or she thought were vitally important to a lasting relationship. They were stymied; they just didn't understand why sparks weren't flying.

The Love Test data uncovered their problem. Angela and Bill both rated each other high on the EMRF, but both rated their romantic attraction low on the RAQ. They just didn't have enough romantic attraction going for them to make a fulfilling relationship.

Disappointed, but relieved, they went ahead with their business partnership and have remained close friends, each supportive of the other's quest for the right love partners.

Can a marriage of convenience give much satisfaction?
It depends on how mature the people in this relationship are. If they have a reasonably high degree of maturity, they will recognize the arrangement for what it is, and they may feel better if they feel the price is right. Some feel that half a loaf is better than no loaf at all. Immature people scream when they have ninety-five percent of a loaf; they want the missing five percent.

Rx for Type-Seven Relationships

Type-Seven lovers can be great friends even though they are not the right partners for marriage. However, if each partner shares high borderline romantic attraction for the other, the benefits of the relationship may be too great to ignore.

- Discuss your ratings. If you are convinced there is too little romantic attraction and few other benefits, look for other partners.
- If your romantic interest is borderline, review your

PERSONAL LOVE PROFILE

Number of Low Scores on
Emotional Maturity Rating
Form (EMRF)

Romantic Attraction
Questionnaire (RAQ) Score

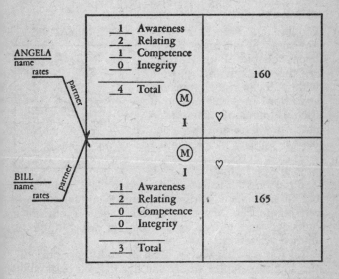

LOVE RELATIONSHIP TYPE_____7_____

Number of low EMRF Scores
0–20 low scores total   M
21 or more low scores total   I

RAQ Scores
♥ 220–300 strong attraction
♥ 200–220 borderline
♡ 180–200 weak attraction

Types of Love Relationships

Type 1 ♥ M ♥ M   Type 4 ♥ M ♡ M   Type 7 ♡ M ♡ M

Type 2 ♥ M ♥ I   [Type 5 ♥ M ♡ I]   Type 8 ♡ M ♡ I
                 [Type 5 ♡ M ♥ I]

Type 3 ♥ I ♥ I   Type 6 ♥ I ♡ I   Type 9 ♡ I ♡ I

benefit/cost ratio carefully before making any decision about your future together.

● No matter what, remain friends!

Type-Eight Relationships: Ships That Pass in the Night

People in a Type-Eight relationship will not make a very happy couple. Both partners are involved with someone without feeling much romantic attraction. In addition, one of them is immature. There is no chemistry here and not much happiness. This couple doesn't belong together and would probably be happier separated.

ONE IS MATURE

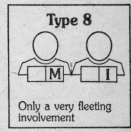

Only a very fleeting involvement

The person who is mature should circulate in the hope of finding someone with whom there is mutual romantic attraction. The immature partner needs professional guidance and a love relationship in which there is mutual attraction.

Jill was a seven-year veteran of poolside potlucks in the singles complex where she lived. Each bash could be the one to which her prince would come. When she saw Fred, a tenant in apartment 212B, at the monthly barbecue, Jill determined she would be open-minded about her prince.

Fred seemed a far cry from her sixteen-year-old version of Prince Charming, but she had grown accustomed to compromising her youthful expectations. Life changes expectations drastically at thirty-one. She cornered Fred by the Jacuzzi and enthusiastically engaged him in conversation. Between his bites of chicken, Fred responded monosyllabically to Jill's zealous questioning. He wasn't much interested and really didn't want to encourage her. However, he agreed to have dinner at her place the next night.

Had these people been sufficiently interested in each other to fill out The Love Test materials, their RAQ scores would have been negligible, and their EMRF scores would have indicated that Jill is living in a fantasy world of teen-age dreams.

After one date with Fred, Jill's determination to make him her next lover waned, and Fred never called again. They returned to their separate lives.

Rx for Type-Eight Relationships

There are very few Type-Eight marriages or lasting relationships because there is little or no romantic attraction on either side and one of the partners is immature. If the romantic attraction for both partners is borderline, there may be grounds for a relationship, and such a couple can do much to improve their relationship.

- Keep rerating each other until you can determine if there is enough romantic attraction to be considered borderline (200 to 220) on *both* sides. If high borderline, there is much you can do to better your relationship. Follow the prescription for Types One and Two.
- If the romantic attraction is below 200, you are better off looking for other partners.
- The person with the immaturity problems should get help in growing up while looking for a new partner. Increased maturity will open up possibilities for better relationships.

PERSONAL LOVE PROFILE

Number of Low Scores on
Emotional Maturity Rating
Form (EMRF)

Romantic Attraction
Questionnaire (RAQ) Score

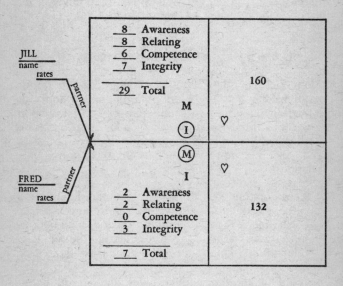

JILL
name
rates

partner

8 Awareness
8 Relating
6 Competence
7 Integrity

29 Total

M

(I)

160

♡

(M)

I

♡

FRED
name
rates

partner

2 Awareness
2 Relating
0 Competence
3 Integrity

7 Total

132

LOVE RELATIONSHIP TYPE_____8_____

Number of low EMRF Scores   *RAQ Scores*
0–20 low scores total   M   ♥ 220–300 strong attraction
21 or more low scores total I   ♥ 200–220 borderline
                                  ♡ 180–200 weak attraction

Types of Love Relationships

Type 1 ♥ M ♥ M	Type 4 ♥ M ♡ M	Type 7 ♡ M ♡ M
Type 2 ♥ M ♥ I	⎡Type 5 ♥ M ♡ I⎤	Type 8 ♡ M ♡ I
	⎣Type 5 ♡ M ♥ I⎦	
Type 3 ♥ I ♥ I	Type 6 ♥ I ♡ I	Type 9 ♡ I ♡ I

Type-Nine Relationships: Ships That Should Pass in the Night

Type Nines have nothing going for them as a partnership. True love eludes them. Both members of the couple are immature and lack romantic excitement.

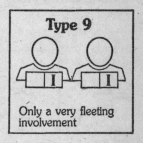

Type 9

Only a very fleeting involvement

At age thirty, Al still doesn't know what he wants to do when he grow up. He drifts from job to job, pulling pennies off the dresser to pay for beers at the beach bar, where he spends most of his time.

At this beach bar, he meets Steffi, the divorced mother of a seven-year-old girl. Loneliness brings them together and, to make ends meet, they decide to take an apartment together and set up housekeeping. Almost immediately, they realize that this is a mistake and separate bitterly. Al considers Steffi and her daughter a terrible burden. He feels they drain him; they expect what he cannot give. Steffi thinks Al should take more responsibility for paying for groceries and keeping up his share of the housekeeping. He's always asking her for beer money!

If Al and Steffi had taken The Love Test, they would have found that their romantic feelings were mutually low and they were both lacking in emotional maturity. Their relationship, a classic Type Nine, is transitory and unfulfilling.

Rx for Type-Nine Relationships

Type-Nine couples have very little going for them. If they are married, they should not separate until they get some help and are better able to establish who they

PERSONAL LOVE PROFILE

Number of Low Scores on
Emotional Maturity Rating
Form (EMRF)

Romantic Attraction
Questionnaire (RAQ) Score

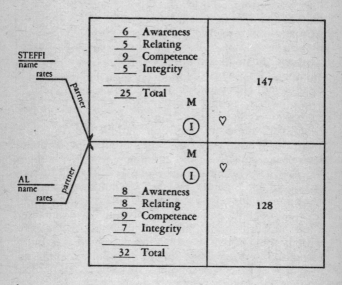

6	Awareness	
5	Relating	
9	Competence	
5	Integrity	
25	Total	147

STEFFI
name
rates

partner

M

Ⓘ   ♡

M

Ⓘ   ♡

AL
name
rates

partner

8	Awareness	
8	Relating	
9	Competence	
7	Integrity	
32	Total	128

LOVE RELATIONSHIP TYPE _____ 9

Number of low EMRF Scores
0–20 low scores total .... M
21 or more low scores total ... I

RAQ Scores
♥ 220–300 strong attraction
♥ 200–220 borderline
♡ 180–200 weak attraction

Types of Love Relationships

Type 1 ♥ M ♥ M   Type 4 ♥ M ♡ M   Type 7 ♡ M ♡ M

Type 2 ♥ M ♥ I   ⎡Type 5 ♥ M ♡ I⎤   Type 8 ♡ M ♡ I
                      ⎣Type 5 ♡ M ♥ I⎦

Type 3 ♥ I ♥ I   Type 6 ♥ I ♡ I   Type 9 ♡ I ♡ I

are and where they're going. Their first decision should be the one to grow up.

- Both partners should seek professional help.
- As partners gain in maturity, ratings should be repeated.
- Increased maturity may help the partners discover *buried* romantic attraction that will surface as they become less fearful. If this happens, follow the tips for Type-Four and Type-One couples.
- If increased maturity does not reveal buried romantic attraction, the couple would be better off looking for new partners. The more emotional maturity gained, the easier will be the search for a new partner and the better the chances for building a Type-One relationship.

Chapter Ten

♡ ♡ ♡

Winning Ways
to Love

You and your partner have used the materials in this book to get a more accurate picture of your romantic attraction to each other and your individual emotional maturity. Your scores have placed you, as a couple, close to one of the nine different types of relationships on the Love Relationships Chart. Some of these relationships can lead to a happier life than others. Some can and should be saved and can become much more fulfilling. Others can be improved tremendously if one partner makes serious efforts to grow up. In relationships where one-way love exists, it will be more difficult to improve your relationship. You may not have a Type-One relationship, but you should review the benefit/cost ratio (see p. 203) to see if there are valuable benefits in your relationship that meaningfully compensate for only moderate excitement or borderline maturity.

You can change and improve your relationship if the problems are those of immaturity. If you are in a Type-Two or Type-Three relationship, you can become a Type-One couple. In fact, if both of you *want* to stay together, and agree to work at your relationship, you will improve your lives together significantly. Separation is only called for when one member of the adamantly refuses to make efforts to improve. But if security is the most important aspect of your relationship, you will probably want to keep what you have!

When *both* people work together, improvement will be assured. When professional help is added, improvement will be made at an even more rapid rate.

Most people are very reluctant to separate. They may admit that they are unhappy; they may agree that their relationship is not very satisfying. They may even confide that they are miserable. Yet a divorce would be out of the question. These people need to admit honestly that for them a poor relationship is better than no relationship. Then they can adopt a better attitude. These couples can decide to work together to make their marriage, and therefore their lives, better. It involves the realization that marriage is not the end of the line of a chain of developments, but the beginning of the line in a life filled with ups and downs. Some marriages *are* mistakes and should end soon. Other marriages can and should be made better by determination and a persistent demonstration of positive personal interest in each other's happiness.

All of us can become more realistic as we strive to become more mature. When we are more realistic, we will have a more reasonable attitude about what can be expected from marriage and be more grateful for what we do have rather than feeling bitter about what we don't have.

Assess Your Prospects

The first thing you need to do now is study The Love Test materials that you and your partner have filled in. Discuss each response, if necessary. Learn why your partner made a specific rating. If you are in a one-way love relationship, you may want to settle for the other benefits this partner has to offer. If you are a Type-Two or Type-Three couple, you have enough romantic attraction on your side. All you need is to gain maturity and yours will become a Type-One relationship.

Analyze your Personal Love Profile and find the most realistic and best possible goal for yourself. Each couple will need to study the total picture before seeing what improvements need to be made.

You Don't Have to Have a Type-One Relationship to Be Reasonably Happy

The goal of all couples is not necessarily to achieve a Type-One relationship. Couples with mutual attraction should be working to develop a Type-One relationship, because they have the potential to have that kind of relationship. I've seen Type-Four and Type-Five couples that are reasonably happy together. *You don't have to have a Type-One relationship to have a reasonably good marriage*. And, if you are a Type-One, you still have to show your partner the consistent, positive, personal interest he or she needs or you can slip into being a Type-One gone astray. Never take each other for granted!

Emotional maturity is such an important part of true love that it deserves to be the first priority of every adult. Once you have gained enough maturity to take a calm and realistic look at your love life, you can make a rational decision about what should come next. If you are already blessed with equally high romantic attraction between your partner and yourself, once you gain maturity, your relationship will become a Type One. Even if your relationship is not one of great romantic attraction, you should find help in gaining more maturity before you walk away from any relationship to seek romance with another partner.

The Love Prescriptions

To get my patients on the right track toward a happier marriage—a more substantial and fulfilling relationship—I suggest they follow doctor's orders for three months. These rules will not change the *basic* degree of romantic attraction, but they will help any couple that is motivated to improve the way they treat each other.

Rx 1: Forget About Fighting

Only Types One and Type Fours can afford to fight, because they are the only ones who are both mature enough to know how to fight constructively. For everyone else, the rule is very simple: There should be no fighting until there is enough maturity to fight constructively.

Fighting usually makes matters worse. No one wins; everyone loses. The logic of the arguments rarely impresses the other partner; the battle of wits in the game of "Do you remember?" is a waste of time because no two people remember the same event in the same way and the conviction that one person's judgment is better than another's is damaging to the team. Fighting usually tends to alienate your partner more— it's like pouring gasoline on an already-burning fire. Instead of fighting, initiate one-to-one time (see pp. 134 and 236) and try some better ways of listening.

Rx 2: Try Really Listening

When you are really listening to your partner's thoughts and feelings, you do not interrupt, overpower, try to outmaneuver, impress, or convince the other of your own viewpoint. Don't utter a word other than to encourage your partner to say everything he has to say on the subject. When it's your turn to talk, your lover must you with the same respect you gave him or

ne cases, you may find that after listening to
yo   artner's views, you may come to understand and
even like his or her solution better than your own! If,
after listening, you still think that your solution is
better, work toward a reasonable and fair compromise
that satisfies each of you.

If winning ego points or controlling your partner is
the most important thing, there is no hope for your
relationship. You are locked into toxic, immature behavior that needs professional attention.

If, however, you can stop fighting and start listening,
you will find that you can start compromising. And, you
will be on your way to a more mature solution to your
problems and a happier life.

Rx 3: Build Trust

Provisional trust can ease the way to a happier lifestyle. Extend a small amount of trust and see what
happens. A lover who has lived with years of frustration
and anguish is naturally wary of his or her partner. Trust
wears thin or even finally wears out. To regain trust,
provisional trust must be offered first.

Provisional trust is extended on a limited basis—for
one time or one week or one month. The lover who is
wary gives his or her partner a chance to become
trustworthy again. Each time the partner comes through,
new trust is gained and a stronger bond is built. Because people in love are willing to forgive, provisional
trust can be the cornerstone of a new and stronger
relationship. But, be sure to ask and give only minisized commitments or contracts in the beginning, because small ones are much easier to fulfill. Improvement,
no matter how small, if it is sincere, will be impressive
and will start to rebuild hope and trust.

Rx 4: Never Underestimate the Power of the Written Word

Written messages between lovers have tremendous value. Leave your wife a note on the refrigerator door. Write your husband a note and put it in his briefcase. Get into the habit of expressing small but sincere sentiments in love-note form. Let your partner know you were thinking of him or her. Let love-note writing become second nature to you. It will only serve to reinforce your love. If one or both of you have developed the bad habit of not listening or not remembering what you heard, you can reopen communication via a new pathway.

Rx 5: Be Sensitive to Your Partner's Moods

Before approaching your partner with a serious issue, a request, complain, or problem, first find out what kind of mood he or she is in. Remember that when a person is in a bad mood and suffers fear, anger, depression, hurt, insecurity, or some similar problem, there is often a high degree of distortion in receiving messages.

Rx 6: Be Honest

It pays to be honest with your partner in all things but one: sexual indiscretion. I have seldom found a confession of infidelity to do any good, and I have seen it do a great deal of harm. This does not reduce the value of honesty, but points out that concern for the feelings of one's partner should outweigh the personal desire to ease guilt feelings through confession. Talking about an indiscretion has no constructive benefits.

Being honest about other painful subjects that can affect the relationship, however, is important. Remember that wounds have to heal in order for your relationship to improve. Do not intentionally bring pain upon your partner, but be honest when it is called for and will be constructive, even if it is momentarily unpleasant.

Almost always my patients say that they want to be fully informed, even if there is some pain.

Rx 7: Share One-to-One Time

Once you have practiced at building the patience necessary for really good listening (without fighting), you will be ready for some one-to-one time.

One-to-one time is an essential element in any working marriage. Take twenty minutes each day, ten uninterrupted minutes per person, and tell each other about your day: what went well, what went poorly, who said what, and so on. This is your time to tune in to your partner and to really listen.

During this time, you each have a license to tell anything you want to the other person (except about past love affairs and marital indiscretions). Talk about whatever you want to talk about, whether it makes you feel good or bad. The hardest part will be for each of you to abstain from responding while the other one is talking. If you are talking or responding, you are not listening properly. Head nodding is fine. But, don't interrupt with questions. It will be difficult in the beginning for you not to become ego-defensive. The issue should not be who is right or wrong. Realize that you will have your own turn and your partner will listen just as fully to you without interruption. As you do this, your listening silently should grow progressively easier.

When you listen, remember that you need not and should not respond defensively. When you say how you feel, you will be reporting *reality as it seems to you*. This is enough. There need not and should not be an argument to see who is right or wrong. The purpose of the one-to-one time is to get to know each other's intimate thoughts and feelings. This builds mutual empathy, an essential factor in every good relationship.

By investing this twenty minutes each day, you will steadily increase your understanding of each other and make it safe to give and receive honest, but always

supportive, confrontation. One-to-one time will fost
deep and genuine mutual empathy that will build you
relationship into one of deep mutual understanding and
appreciation. One-to-one sessions will build a sympa-
thetic understanding of the other person's needs and
how those needs can be best fulfilled.

Rx 8: Let Your Lover Support Your Efforts Toward Maturity

While professional therapy can provide substantial help,
you can and should get real therapeutic benefit from
your lover as well. In relationships that are Type One,
Two, Four, and Five, the mature partner is often capable of helping the other partner. In Type-Three
relationships, each partner will first have to develop the
constructive skills of a mature person to help the other
since both need professional help. But, they can still
help each other as they become more mature.

An inevitable part of growing up is getting hurt and,
once burned, we tend to be twice shy. We want love,
affection, sex, and belonging, and yet we are subconsciously wary of the pain of rejection.

When we are romantically attracted, we attempt
some kind of balancing act. We relate, involve ourselves,
but we hedge our investment; we hold back. This
creates a terrible problem because our holding back is
interpreted by our partners not as self-protection but as
rejection.

This misinterpretation can and should be corrected,
but success requires mutual romantic interest and sufficient emotional maturity. A marriage counselor can
help to ask the right questions, give the correct
information, help map out effective strategies, but only
a lover can actually *give* the loving and reassurance
needed. The lovers are going to be together in the
kitchen, the living room, and the bedroom; only they
will have the hundreds of opportunities to show each
other the security of their special closeness.

Rx 9: Practice Bessell's Ten Rules of Togetherness

Bessell's Ten Rules of Togetherness are practiced by all Type Ones. Even if your relationship is not a Type One, by practicing these additional rules you will see improvements in your love relationship. If you are unable to put these growth-inducing methods into your lifestyle, you will not have a very good chance of improvement.

It is possible for people to change, and as you and/or your partner change, your love relationship will also change. As you integrate the tips in this book into your life, use the RAQ and EMRF tests in chapters two and three to rerate your maturity. Within a few weeks, you will see an improvement in some of your emotional maturity scores.

To be sure of continuing results, rerate each other's emotional maturity each month.

The Lag Factor

When you see a person every day, small changes may escape your notice: a weight loss, a change of attitude, an improvement in behavior. As one partner changes, there is a strong tendency for the other partner to be blind to these changes. The partner tends to continue to perceive his or her lover in the old fixed picture, to see with eyes of the past. This phenomenon is called the Lag Factor, and if not accounted for, the efforts toward change may go unnoticed. And caring treatment that is not noticed is, to a large extent, wasted.

To counteract the Lag Factor, you will need to let your partner know that you are changing. Not only must your behavior change as a consequence of your newfound emotional maturity, but you must *tell* your partner that you are being more attentive or affectionate, that you are listening better, that you are being more honest.

Without telling your partner of your changes, it may take several months for your new behavior to be noticed. You will get little reinforcement until your improved behavior is recognized.

Living Happier Ever After

By devoting yourself to looking after your partner's very best interests, you will be looking after your own well-being in the best of all possible ways. When this philosophical attitude is mutual and the commitment is not only stated but demonstrated every day of your lives, your relationship will assuredly survive and it will also flourish. When we know what we are doing, appreciate what we have, emphasize the positives in our lives, we are wisely devoting ourselves to the most important thing in life—that meaningful relationship that will bring us the richness and fulfillment that we all seek and deserve.

Bibliography

Readings on Romance, Maturity, Sex, Marriage, and Divorce

Bessell, Harold, *The Maturity Kit*. La Jolla, Calif.: Psych/Graphic Publishers, 1978. A scientific approach to measuring emotional maturity in the school setting, with specific guidance for fostering emotional maturity by the classroom teacher.

——, and Thomas P. Kelly. *The Parent Book*. Rolling Hills Estates, Calif.: Jalmar Press, 1977. A comprehensive description of what emotional maturity is and how the parent stimulates and challenges its development in the child. Available from B. L. Winch & Associates, Rolling Hills Estates, Calif. 90274.

Colgrove, Melba, Harold H. Bloomfield, and Peter McWilliams. *How to Survive the Loss of a Love*. New York: Bantam Books, 1976. Realistic, effective ways to survive the inevitable depression following the loss of love.

Dowling, Collette. *The Cinderella Complex: Women's Hidden Fear of Independence*. New York: Pocket Books, 1981. A lucid account of many women's conflicts and dilemmas: to become emotionally mature and independent or to remain immature and pay all the prices required. Must reading for every female who wants to become a true adult.

240

Friday, Nancy. *Men in Love. Male Sexual Fantasies: The Triumph of Love Over Rage*. New York: Delacorte, 1980. A very compassionate presentation of men's sexual fantasies. It shows the very reasonable basis for men's resentment toward women (enticing yet forbidden), the basis for ambivalence (love and hate), and what men really want and need in lovemaking.

———. *My Mother, My Self: The Daughter's Search for Identity*. New York: Delacorte, 1977. A simple, excellent, and exceedingly accurate and detailed description of the negative and positive aspects of a young girl's development of her concept of herself as a female in our often misguided culture.

Gellis, Audrey. *How to Meet Men Now That You're Liberated*. New York: Popular Library, 1978. Gives specific ideas and encouragement for meeting potential new partners.

Greenwald, Jerry A. *Creative Intimacy*. New York: Simon and Schuster, 1975. Describes nourishing and toxic personalities and shows how toxic personality traits antagonize a partner and create undesirable distance in the love relationship. Shows how to recognize and deal with toxic behavior in your love partner.

Horney, Karen. *Neurosis and Human Growth: The Struggle Toward Self-Realization*. New York: W. W. Norton & Co., 1950. Shows clearly and succinctly the hidden fears, distortions, and expectations characteristic of people who hedge on their relating with three kinds of "safety through distancing" devices. Explicitly shows the internal wars between the idealized self and the real self. You will find almost everyone you know described to some extent in this book. It will help you to learn who you are dealing with and the probable reasons for behavior.

Krantzler, Mel. *Creative Divorce*. New York: New American Library, Signet Books, 1974. A personal account of the emotional strains and turmoil of adjusting to a divorce, living alone, and the challenge and opportunity of starting over with a new and better relationship.

Murstein, Bernard I. *Love, Sex, and Marriage Through the Ages*. New York: Springer Publishing Co., 1974. A responsible and scholarly history of the male-female relationship, showing how it has been modified over time through changes in society, religion, education, transportation, affluence, and the Industrial Revolution.

Peele, Stanton, with Archie Brodsky. *Love and Addiction*. New York: Taplinger Publishing Co., 1975. Discusses in great detail the price many people are willing to pay in order not to be alone, to believe they belong to someone.

Powell, John. *The Secret of Staying in Love*. Allen, Tex.: Argus Communications, 1974. Discusses the importance of making a deep, permanent commitment to the one you love.

———. *Why Am I Afraid to Tell You Who I Am?* Allen, Tex.: Argus Communications, 1969. Easy-to-understand guidance on how to improve self-awareness, emotional maturity, and interpersonal communications.

Sherfey, Mary Jane. *The Nature and Evolution of Female Sexuality*. New York: Random House, 1973. An understanding and clear description of how the female orgasm happens, its anatomy and physiology, plus a historical discussion of society's suppression of female sexuality.

Short, Ray E. *Sex, Love, or Infatuation: How Can I Really Know?* Minneapolis: Augsburg Publishing House, 1978. Valuable and pertinent research on love and infatuation. Provides a moral guide to choosing a partner on a wise and realistic basis, having realistic expectations, and building mature love. Helps to differentiate sex from love and infatuation from love.

Zilbergeld, Bernie. *Male Sexuality: A Guide to Sexual Fulfillment*. New York: Bantam Books, 1978. An excellent discussion of male sexual interest and dysfunctions and what to do about them. Could easily be the best treatise on male sexuality yet written. Deals with many common myths about sex.